Project® 2013

ABSOLUTE BEGINNER'S GUIDE

Brian Kennemer and Sonia Atchison

800 East 96th Street,
Indianapolis, Indiana 46240

Project 2013 Absolute Beginner's Guide

ISBN-13: 978-0-7897-5055-6
ISBN-10: 0-7897-5055-4

Library of Congress Control Number: 2013937702

Printed in the United States of America

First Printing: July 2013

Trademarks

All terms mentioned in this book that are known to be trademarks or service marks have been appropriately capitalized. Que Publishing cannot attest to the accuracy of this information. Use of a term in this book should not be regarded as affecting the validity of any trademark or service mark.

Warning and Disclaimer

Every effort has been made to make this book as complete and as accurate as possible, but no warranty or fitness is implied. The information provided is on an "as is" basis. The author and the publisher shall have neither liability nor responsibility to any person or entity with respect to any loss or damages arising from the information contained in this book or from the use of the programs accompanying it.

Bulk Sales

Que Publishing offers excellent discounts on this book when ordered in quantity for bulk purchases or special sales. For more information, please contact

U.S. Corporate and Government Sales
1-800-382-3419
corpsales@pearsontechgroup.com

For sales outside the United States, please contact

International Sales
international@pearsoned.com

Associate Publisher
Greg Wiegand

Executive Editor
Loretta Yates

Development Editor
Brandon Cackowski-Schnell

Managing Editor
Sandra Schroeder

Project Editor
Seth Kerney

Copy Editor
Keith Cline

Indexer
Brad Herriman

Proofreader
Debbie Williams

Technical Editor
Sonia Atchison

Publishing Coordinator
Cindy Teeters

Book Designer
Anne Jones

Compositor
Mary Sudul

Contents at a Glance

Table of Contents

About the Authors

Brian Kennemer has been working with Project since 1997 and is a part of the Microsoft MVP program for Project and Project Server. He was on the Microsoft Consulting Services Global Enterprise Project Management team for five years and has also worked for several different Microsoft Partners, specializing in the design and deployment of Project Server-based project management systems. He was recognized in 2012 as a Microsoft MVP for Project and Project Server. He lives in Washington state with his amazing wife and three incredible kids.

Sonia Atchison has been working with Microsoft Project since 1999. In 2006, she joined the writing team at Microsoft that produces Help content and videos for Project and Project Server, planning and writing Office.com and TechNet content for the 2007, 2010, and 2013 releases.

Acknowledgments

Brian: I want to thank the entire Pearson/Que team for their tireless editing that makes me seem like a better writer than I really am. Everyone thanks their spouse in these things, but in my case it is doubly appropriate. Not only has Alicia Kennemer supported me in the effort to write this book, but it was also her encouragement that allowed me to make a career change back in 1999 that put me on the path to become as knowledgeable as I am about Microsoft Project and Project Server. Without her, I don't even want to think about where I would be. Thanks, Alicia.

Sonia: For their unending patience, thanks to Vince, Jasper, and Courtney Atchison, and to Brian Kennemer and Loretta Yates.

We Want to Hear from You!

As the reader of this book, *you* are our most important critic and commentator. We value your opinion and want to know what we're doing right, what we could do better, what areas you'd like to see us publish in, and any other words of wisdom you're willing to pass our way.

We welcome your comments. You can email or write us directly to let us know what you did or didn't like about this book—as well as what we can do to make our books better.

Please note that we cannot help you with technical problems related to the topic of this book.

When you write, please be sure to include this book's title and author as well as your name, email address, and phone number. We will carefully review your comments and share them with the authors and editors who worked on the book.

Email: feedback@quepublishing.com

Mail: Que Publishing
       ATTN: Reader Feedback
       800 East 96th Street
       Indianapolis, IN 46240 USA

Reader Services

Visit our website and register this book at http://quepublishing.com/title/9780789750556 using for convenient access to any updates, downloads, or errata that might be available for this book.

- How this book is organized
- Conventions used in this book

INTRODUCTION

Project management is a broad term that can mean something very formal and specific to one person but something very organic and pieced-together to another. The fact of the matter is that "pieced-together" can only get you so far. Spreadsheets, sticky notes, and email are all great tools, and they may work fine for your smaller projects. However, once you start adding just a few more people to a project, or just one or two more reports to generate for upper management, the blood pressure goes up a smidge. Gathering bits and pieces from the various tools you've been using to track your projects gets to be more tedious than you may have time for.

Microsoft Project 2013 addresses these issues gracefully and powerfully. I can't lie: it has a steep learning curve, but it's absolutely worth your time to figure it out, even at a rudimentary level. The amount of time it will ultimately save you is reason enough, and as you complete projects, you can review the project data to help make decisions about future projects. It's a thing of beauty, really, especially if you've been used to a lot of manual updating and high-maintenance project and resource tracking.

Project 2013 is versatile enough to help bring order to a novice project manager's plans while offering rich solutions for experienced project managers. The experienced user will benefit from things such as earned value and critical path analysis, resource leveling, and heavy customizability to meet organizational needs while the product also provides the simple, easy-to-use features to manage even the smallest efforts.

How This Book Is Organized

This book introduces you to Project 2013. It is designed to familiarize you with project management terminology, as it is used in Project 2013, and covers functionality that was brought forward from earlier versions of Project, as well as features that are new in Project 2013. This book is far from a be-all end-all reference book for Project 2013. Instead, it focuses on introducing the concepts and procedures that are most commonly used. *Project 2013 Absolute Beginner's Guide* does the following:

- It goes over some high-level project management theory as it applies to Project 2013.

- It introduces features that are new in this version.

- It orients you to Project 2013, including the different parts of the Project window and the many views available to you.

- It walks you through the process of creating a project, from adding tasks and assigning resources, to tracking costs and reporting on progress.

- It touches on some simple customization options, as a starting point for more advanced topics.

- It offers some solutions to commonly encountered project issues.

Conventions Used in This Book

Here's a quick look at a few structural features designed to help you get the most out of this book.

TIP   A *tip* is a piece of advice—a little trick, actually—that helps you more effectively maneuver around problems or limitations.

NOTE   A *note* is designed to provide information that is generally useful but not specifically necessary for what you're doing at the moment. Some are like extended tips—interesting, but not essential.

CAUTION   A *caution* tells you to beware of a potentially dangerous act or situation. In some cases, ignoring a caution could cause you significant problems—so pay attention to them!

INTRODUCTION TO MANAGING PROJECTS WITH MICROSOFT PROJECT 2013

This chapter helps you understand what Project 2013 does as an application, and how it can help you do your job of tracking your work efforts. It also reviews the basic elements of the Project 2013 data structure (tasks, resources, assignments), as well as going over what is new and improved in the 2013 version.

So here's a common scenario: You've been put in charge of a major project in your organization. The project started off pretty straightforward but has grown too big for the system of sticky notes and spreadsheets that has always worked for smaller past projects. The number of tasks and the complexity with which these tasks are connected and depend on each other along with the way resources need to work together on the tasks has made this one the most complicated effort you have ever managed. Shifting task finish dates, varying team member work schedules, and increasing or decreasing scope all work together to make you think about escape! How do you figure out where your project actually *is* with regard to schedule and status? When someone asks, "So, when is this thing going to be finished?" how do you answer?

This is the point where you, as a project manager, can either throw your hands up and start planning that escape, or you can step up to the plate and take your project scheduling skills to the next level. What's the next level? Tools. My preference? Microsoft Project 2013.

What Microsoft Project 2013 Can Do for You

Microsoft Project 2013 is a software tool that takes a lot of the manual updating and guesswork out of managing your projects. You can enter information about all the things that need to happen during your project, when they need to happen, the order in which they need to happen, how long you think they should take, and who should be doing the work. As you make updates to your project, Project 2013's scheduling engine takes all project work and availability of people and materials into account, providing a grounded schedule that represents the reality of what can be accomplished. Once you've seen the facts, you can move forward and make adjustments to the time, scope, or costs involved with your project, to find an acceptable solution. Think of it as building a model of your schedule.

 NOTE Not sure how to adjust your project to meet certain constraints? Consider the project management triangle: one side each for time, scope, and costs associated with your project. If you have fewer people working on the project than you had planned, make up for that by extending the project deadline or by backing off on what your project is trying to get done. If you have a smaller budget than planned, adjust your project by not doing quite as much work or by allowing more time to get the work done. If your project expands to include more work, increase the budget to hire more people or extend the schedule so that the people currently assigned to the project have more time to finish the added work.

As your project progresses, things will change. Some tasks will finish earlier, some later, some team members will be added, some removed. Tasks you did not think of will get added or the project scope may increase. Having a model of your project in Microsoft Project 2013 allows you to make small adjustments to your model to see how these changes impact the finish date of the project or the workloads of the team members. You can also use the model to work out different what-if type scenarios. What if your boss wants the whole thing done a week sooner? What if a key resource gets moved to a new project? What if a key deliverable takes longer to complete?

When your manager knocks on your door asking for a status report in the next 10 minutes, you can use the new reporting features in Project 2013 to quickly produce several different impactful and visually attractive reports, showing overall project health, budget tracking, and earned value over time. And you'll already know what the reports will reveal, because each time you make changes in your project, the charts and views that illustrate your project work over time are updated in real time. No surprises!

Laying a Foundation

Before we get started talking about the details of using Project 2013, we need to be clear on a few terms because they're used extensively in the Project 2013 interface.

Project

Just so we're clear, when we talk about projects in relation to Project 2013, a *project* is a set of work that is completed according to a schedule and that has some kind of end result. For example, a project may result in a tangible item, such as a report, a building, or a retail product, or it may result in an intangible item, such as an event, a set of goals, or a strategy. The traditional definition would also say that a project is a one-time effort but as the principles of project management become more and more popular and better understood, those principles and management tools also seem to be getting used on work efforts that might not fit this traditional definition. Some organizations use Project 2013 to track and manage ongoing manufacturing work or IT support efforts. These do not meet the traditional definition of a project, but you can still use Project 2013 to assist with these efforts. The key point here is to not get caught up in the strict definition of *project* when thinking about where you can use a tool like Project 2013.

Task

A *task* is a smaller chunk of work that contributes to the completion of a project. For example, if you're planning a project to build a house, you will have separate tasks for laying the foundation, putting up the walls, and adding the roof. In Project 2013, each task has a start date and a finish date, and you can assign people/things to help do the task work.

Resource

A *resource* can be a person, an item or facility, or an expense that is required to complete the work associated with a task. In Project 2013, people are referred to as work resources, items such as network cable or building supplies are referred to as *material resources*, and expenses or other costs are referred to as *cost resources*. A single task may require more than one type of resource. For example, if the task is to travel to a satellite office and install networking equipment, you might need a person (work resource) to do the installation, a round-trip plane ticket (cost resource) to get the person to and from the satellite office, and network cabling (material resource).

 NOTE Equipment that is required for a task is often represented using work resources because equipment often needs to have a schedule just like a human resource.

Assignment

An *assignment* is the link between a resource and a task. When you want a certain resource to work on a task, you assign that resource to the task in Project 2013. A task can have many different resources assigned, but each one might work different amounts of time or might work at different times. Each of these resources has its own assignment for the task.

The Project 2013 Version You Need

Project 2013 comes in two versions: Standard and Professional. Project Standard has all the basic functionality to track and manage even complex projects. The Professional version adds a few features that are generally used by more advanced users, users who use Project much more often than a casual user or by managers who will be working with projects in a collaborative environment such as SharePoint, Office 365, or Project Server. If you manage a few projects and find that you do not need the collaboration features or the more advanced features covered here, the Standard edition should work for you just fine. If you are working in a shared environment or you find yourself managing many projects or working with more complex resource management situations, however, the Professional version might work better for you.

Subscribers to some plans within Office365 will also have access to Project Professional 2013 through their Office365 sites. Even though it is accessed in a different way, it is the same product, and all the things covered in this book still apply.

What's New in Project 2013?

This section covers what is new to 2013 and reviews the things that were added to Project 2010, as well, just in case you are moving from 2003 or 2007 directly to 2013.

Updated User Interface

Although the ribbon is not new to Project 2013 (it was added to Project in the 2010 version), if you are coming to 2013 from a pre-2010 version it will be new to you. Gone are the old menus with lists of commands. Commands that had previously been available in the menus at the top of the Project window are now available as buttons on several tabs across the top of each view, as shown in Figure 1.1.

FIGURE 1.1

The ribbon is displayed at the top of the Project window and displays the most commonly used commands in easy-to-navigate tabs and groups.

In Project 2013, the ribbon tabs display commonly used commands for the different types of things you are doing in the application. For example, if you're making changes to the way the **Gantt Chart** view is displayed, an entire tab with buttons controls what bars are displayed, what colors are used, and other formatting options.

Manually Scheduled Tasks (Professional and Standard)

Up until Project 2010, tasks could only be scheduled using Project's built-in scheduling engine. That is, you'd tell Project a few details about a task, such as when it should start and how long it should take (duration), and Project would figure out when the task would be done, based on how many resources were assigned to the task, what other things (constraints, task dependencies) the task depended on, and what the calendar looked like. Until you had a good understanding of how Project was making these calculations, the scheduling engine seemed to be a bit of a mystery. (Don't worry, though; we demystify this a bit later in the book.) Even some experienced project managers who had been using Project for years would occasionally run into situations in complex projects where the dates given by the scheduling engine were just not what they expected.

Starting with Project 2010, Microsoft has added a new way to schedule tasks by introducing *manually scheduled tasks*. That is, instead of always allowing Project 2013 to calculate when a task should start or finish, you can identify a task as being manually scheduled, and then you have full control over task start and finish dates.

Team Planner View (Professional Only)

The **Team Planner** view, available only in Project Professional 2013, is a quick, easy, and highly visual way of reviewing and changing what your team members are working on in your project. As shown in Figure 1.2, you can see where people may have too much on their plates (overallocation), what tasks have yet to be assigned, and what the current progress is on your project's tasks.

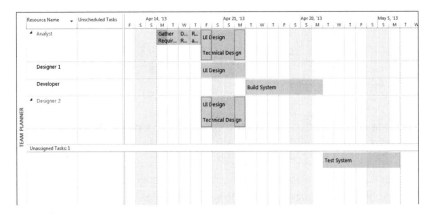

FIGURE 1.2

The Team Planner view shows what each team member is working on.

You can resolve overallocations by dragging tasks between team members and assign tasks to people by dragging them from the **Unassigned Tasks** area of this view to a team member's name.

Timeline (Professional and Standard)

Added in 2010 and improved in 2013, the timeline allows you to create presentation-ready summary graphics of key tasks on your project.

At the top of each view, you can display a timeline of your project, illustrating project tasks and dates (see Figure 1.3).

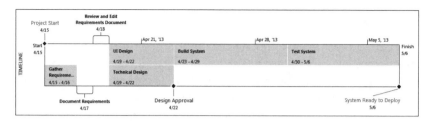

FIGURE 1.3

The timeline is a great way to display task information in an easy-to-digest format for presentations.

The timeline is a great way to summarize task information for presentations or even emails. This format is often easier to understand than a Gantt chart and can help others in your organization see the basic flow of your project. It can be easily copied into other applications for sharing with those who are interested in your project.

Task Path (Professional and Standard)

New to Project 2013 is the Task Path feature. One of the key features that makes Project useful to you as a project manager is the ability to link tasks together to show the order in which tasks need to occur. In a large project, these links can become a bit confusing, particularly when trying to figure out which tasks are linked either directly or indirectly to a specific task in the project. The Task Path feature enables you to apply different Gantt bar formatting to tasks that are linked to a selected task. Figure 1.4 shows this formatting. The tasks colored orange are the driving predecessors for Task 5, and the purple are the driven successors. Notice that Task 4 is also a predecessor of Task 5, but because a gap of time occurs between its finish date and Task 5 start date, it is not colored as a driving predecessor.

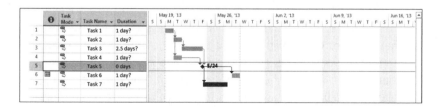

FIGURE 1.4

The Task Path feature provides quick visibility of the tasks that affect or are affected by a selected task.

Reporting (Professional and Standard)

Project 2013 provides a complete overhaul of the reporting features within Project. The new reports are easier to understand, and enable you to efficiently gain and share insight about your project. In addition, it provides a set of design tools for building your own custom reports that can include filtered and grouped tables, data graphics, and shapes that enable you to display key data in a way that is easy to understand for you and your project stakeholders.

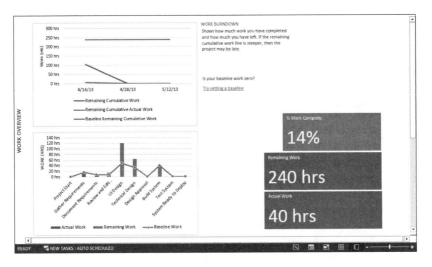

FIGURE 1.5

The Work Overview report shows the state of work on the project.

Inactive Tasks (Professional Only)

Project 2010 added the concept of an inactive task. This is a task or set of tasks that you create just like any other task and then you mark them as inactive. Marking them as inactive leaves them in your project but removes them from the scheduling engine so that they don't impact the schedule. The best example of this is having a set of tasks in your project that is only there to represent what you will do if some event occurs. Your project is the planning of an event, and you know that it might rain on the day of your event. You can create a whole set of tasks related to putting up awnings or moving the event into a nearby building. You can link them together with the other tasks and then mark them as inactive. With them marked this way, they do not impact the schedule, but you can mark them as active again to see how rain might affect the rest of your schedule.

SharePoint Collaboration (Professional Only)

If you have Project Professional 2013, you can export your project to a SharePoint project tasks list, which is included as part of SharePoint Foundation. This enables you to share project information without Project Server 2013 and without requiring others to have Project 2013 installed.

THE ABSOLUTE MINIMUM

Project 2013 is a great tool for managing your work and resource loads, and comes in two versions, Standard and Professional. Choose Professional if you are working with Project Server, or if you need some of the more advanced features that only appear in Professional.

IN THIS CHAPTER

- Getting around Project 2013
- Commonly used views
- Customizing Project 2013 views

2

NAVIGATING PROJECT 2013

This chapter helps you understand the most commonly used views in Project 2013 and how to customize the data displayed in those views to best suit your needs.

The first step in really digging into Project 2013 is to look closely at the different parts of the user interface. At the top of the Project window is the ribbon, below that is the timeline, and below the timeline is the view display area.

Using the Ribbon

The ribbon is made up of several *tabs* that display commands appropriate for whatever view you're using in Project 2013. Each tab contains several *groups* of buttons, separated by vertical gray lines and labeled in gray text at the bottom of the tab. Figure 2.1 illustrates the tabs and groups on the ribbon.

FIGURE 2.1

The ribbon is displayed at the top of the Project window.

The **Task**, **Resource**, **Project**, and **View** tabs are always available, with some buttons on each tab unavailable depending on what view you're using or what is selected. For example, if you are in the **Resource Sheet** view and you have the **Task** tab selected, most of the buttons in the **Schedule** group on that tab will be disabled because they are valid only when working with tasks.

Each view in Project 2013 has a special **Format** tab with buttons for commands that you can only do in each view. This special tab is the last one on the right, and is highlighted using a different color for each view. In Figure 2.1 you can see the **Gantt Chart Tools Format** tab.

NOTE   The ribbon takes up a good amount of real estate in the Project 2013 window. If you find yourself needing just a little more room to display your project, press **Ctrl+F1** to minimize the ribbon. When the ribbon is minimized, only the tab names appear at the top of the window. When you click a tab name, the ribbon drops down. When you click a command or outside of the ribbon, the ribbon goes back to being minimized. Press **Ctrl+F1** again to bring the ribbon back to its normal "pinned" state.

If you're familiar with previous versions of Project, the interactive ribbon mapping guides available on Office.com can help you find menu commands on the ribbon. To view the Project 2013 interactive guide, go to <INSERT URL HERE>, and then click **Open the Project guide**, under **Use an interactive guide to find my commands**. A printable guide is also available on that page, if you'd prefer a desk reference.

Understanding Project Views

Project 2013 has 27 built-in views that you can use to see different information about your project. Although this might seem like a big number, you will likely spend most of your time in three to five of these views. There are views that display *task* information, such as task names and dates, views that display *resource* information, such as names and rates for the people involved with your project, and views that display *assignment* information, such as what tasks a specific person is working on at a given time.

AVAILABLE VIEWS IN PROJECT 2013

We are not going to go through all 27 built-in views and examine details of how they are used and why you would use each one. What is provided here is a description of the views you will use most often and some examples of how to customize views using the options on the **Gantt Chart Tools Formatting** ribbon tab.

Gantt Chart

This is the view that most people think of when they think about Project (or any scheduling tool, for that matter). Tasks and summary tasks are shown in a table on the left side of the screen, and a bar chart representation of how the tasks fall across time is shown on the right side of the screen. It is great for building out your task list and outlines your tasks into a solid work breakdown structure. It is also one of the best views for seeing your tasks in relation to time. Through sorting, grouping, and filtering the **Gantt Chart** view (see Figure 2.2) provides a great base view to see tasks that are behind schedule, how tasks are performing against their original estimates, and where tasks are in comparison to the critical path.

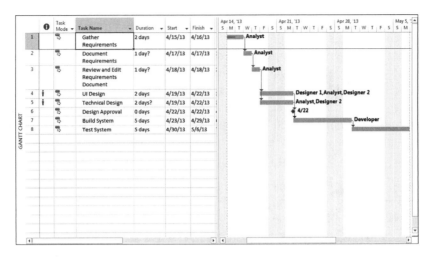

FIGURE 2.2

The Gantt Chart view is a great general purpose view for viewing and editing your project schedule.

Resource Sheet

The **Resource Sheet** view (see Figure 2.3) is the central place for all things resource related. Here you can view basic information about your resources and get to the specific details about each resource, including the specific calendar of their work hour schedule and their pay rate information. It also shows you if the resource is overallocated (assigned to more hours than they are allowed to work) by showing an indicator in the leftmost column and highlighting them in red.

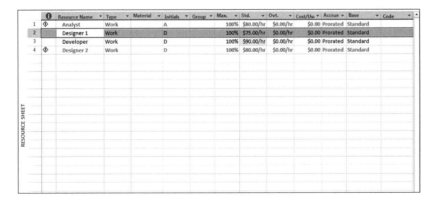

FIGURE 2.3

The Resource Sheet view provides basic information about your project's resources and access to the details about each resource.

Network Diagram

If you have ever taken a project management course in which you learned about calculating the critical path of a set of tasks, the **Network Diagram** view (see Figure 2.4) will be instantly familiar. This view is great for visualizing the links between large sets of tasks, but it is less effective for looking at tasks and how they fall across time. If you need to trace out how tasks relate to each other through their links, this is the view to use.

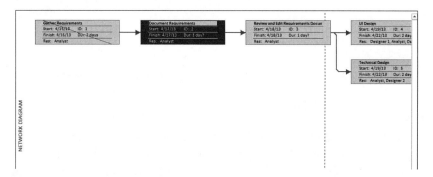

FIGURE 2.4

The Network Diagram view shows how tasks are linked together.

Team Planner

The **Team Planner** view (see Figure 2.5) is available only in the Professional version of Project 2013. It is a bit like a **Gantt Chart** view in that there is a bar chart on the right side that represents tasks across time, but it is different in that the rows on the left side are resources and the bars in the bar chart are the tasks to which they are assigned. It is an extremely useful view for helping you understand how workloads are stacking up over time for a given resource. Not only does it help you see whether a resource has more than one task assigned at the same time, but it also makes it easy to see when a resource has gaps in their assignments. This is key when you are trying to maximize your resource utilization. Knowing when a given resource is finished with all their work lets you know when they can start other tasks or move to other projects. This view also makes it easy to move a task from one resource to another because you can drag the bar for a given task from one resource to another to reassign the task.

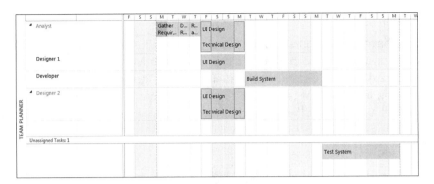

FIGURE 2.5

The Team Planner view provides wonderful insight into resource workloads.

Task Usage

The super-useful **Task Usage** view (see Figure 2.6) is basically just a very detailed form of a Gantt chart. On the left side a table shows two levels of data. On the first level are the tasks, and then indented below the tasks are the names of the resources assigned to that task. On the right side is a timescaled area just like in a Gantt chart. Instead of bars, though, it displays numeric data about the task or assignment. So, for a task that starts on a Monday and has a 5-day duration that is assigned to 1 resource for 8 hours a day instead of a 5-day-long bar like in the Gantt chart, it shows 5 days of 8h in each day, showing the hours assigned to the resource for each of the days.

This is a great view if you need to get the full details on how resources are working across time and how different resources on the same task are working together. Here you can do some serious fine-tuning as well as get a detailed look at how the Project 2013 scheduling engine is doing its work.

	❶	Task Mode ▾	Task Name ▾	Work ▾	Duration ▾	Start ▾	Details	Apr 14, '13 S	M	T	W	T	F	S
1			◢ Gather Requirement	16 hrs	2 days	4/15/13	Work		8h	8h				
			Analyst	16 hrs		4/15/13	Work		8h	8h				
2			◢ Document Requirem	8 hrs	1 day?	4/17/13	Work				8h			
			Analyst	8 hrs		4/17/13	Work				8h			
3			◢ Review and Edit Req	8 hrs	1 day?	4/18/13	Work					8h		
			Analyst	8 hrs		4/18/13	Work					8h		
4	ⓘ		◢ UI Design	48 hrs	2 days	4/19/13	Work						24h	
			Analyst	16 hrs		4/19/13	Work						8h	
			Designer 1	16 hrs		4/19/13	Work						8h	
			Designer 2	16 hrs		4/19/13	Work						8h	
5	ⓘ		◢ Technical Design	32 hrs	2 days?	4/19/13	Work						16h	
			Analyst	16 hrs		4/19/13	Work						8h	
			Designer 2	16 hrs		4/19/13	Work						8h	
6			Design Approval	0 hrs	0 days	4/22/13	Work							
7			◢ Build System	40 hrs	5 days	4/23/13	Work							
			Developer	40 hrs		4/23/13	Work							
8			Test System	0 hrs	5 days	4/30/13	Work							
							Work							

FIGURE 2.6

For full details on workloads for each task, check out the Task Usage view.

Resource Usage

The **Resource Usage** view (see Figure 2.7) is the same as the **Task Usage** view except that the first level of indentation is the name of the resource and the second level is the name of the tasks assigned to that resource. Where the **Task Usage** view is key in helping you understand how resources are working on a task, the **Resource Usage** view is great for letting you see the workloads for a specific resource over time. If you have a resource that is overallocated (assigned more work than they can work on in a given time period), the **Resource Usage** view can be a big help in figuring out exactly where the work is stacking up.

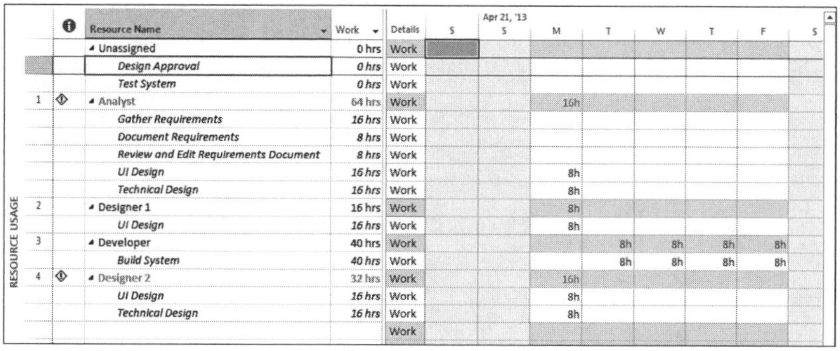

FIGURE 2.7

The Resource Usage view can prove very helpful when trying to level out resource workloads.

Task Form

The **Task Form** view (see Figure 2.8) is generally used as the lower portion of a combination view. It displays several different kinds of information, such as the start and finish dates, duration, task type, % complete, resources assigned, predecessors and successors, and so on. This data is displayed in an easy-to-read form type of format.

FIGURE 2.8

Use the Task Form view to view many task level details in one compact form-type view.

Working with Project Views

After you've decided which view you want to use while working with your project, the next step is to think about how to display the data in that view. Project 2013 allows you to group, sort, filter, highlight, or split the view so that you are looking at the right set of data for whatever you're trying to accomplish.

Grouping Data in a View

When you group data in a view, you display all tasks or resources with a common factor together. For example, in the **Resource Sheet** view, you might find it helpful to group the resources by **Type**, so that all work resources are displayed together, all material resources are displayed together, and all cost resources are displayed together. Figure 2.9 shows what this type of grouping looks like.

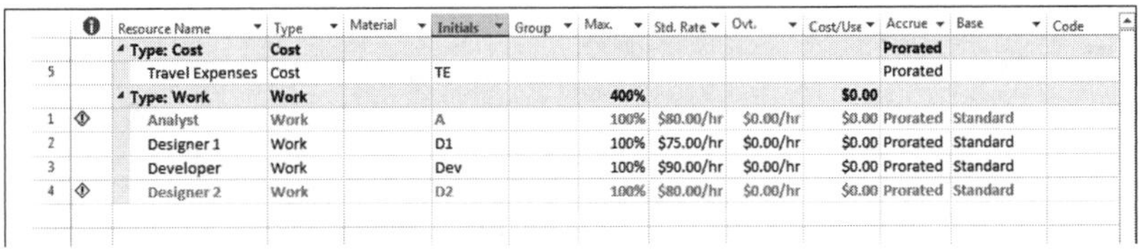

FIGURE 2.9

Grouping provides an easy way to view sets of resources or tasks displayed together onscreen.

You can group data in a view in two different ways. If the field you want to group by is displayed in the view, click the arrow on the right side of the column header, click **Group on this field**, and Project will group the view by that field.

You can also group the data in a view using the ribbon, as follows:

1. On the **View** tab of the ribbon, in the **Data** group, choose the criterion that you want to use to group data from the **Group By** list.

2. If the criterion that you want to group by is not listed, click **More Groups** if you think the grouping is already set up, or click **New Group By** to set up a new grouping.

3. To set up a new grouping, on the **Group Definition** dialog box (see Figure 2.10), complete the following:

   - **Name:** Give the grouping a name.

   - **Show in menu:** Select this check box to display the grouping in the **Group By** list.

- **Group By:** Click the **Field Name** column in the **Group By** row, and then click the name of the first field you want to group by. Click the **Order** column in the **Group By** row to choose whether you want the data in the field you selected to be displayed in **Ascending** or **Descending** order.

- **Then By:** Complete each Then By row, as needed, to create subgroups within each group. For example, if you chose to group by **Type**, in a resource view, you might find it helpful to create a subgroup within that group, to sort by **Base Calendar**. This would show all work resources, for example, that use a night shift calendar, together in a resource view.

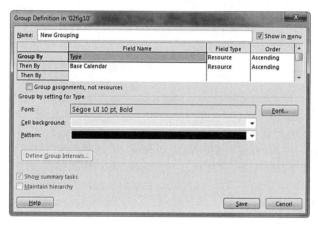

FIGURE 2.10

Creating a multilevel grouping can make large, complex views easier to read.

4. Use the plus or minus signs next to the group rollups to expand or collapse each group.

5. Click **Clear Group** in the **Group By** list to remove the grouping from the view.

Sorting Data in a View

By sorting data in a view, you choose the order in which you want data to appear. For example, you may want a list of names to be displayed in order from A to Z, or you may want a list of dates to be displayed from earliest to latest. There are two ways to sort data in a view. If the data you want to sort is displayed in the view, you can click the arrow on the right side of the column header, and then choose the sort option from the list that appears. For example, if I click the arrow on the right side of the **Duration** column header, I can choose to **Sort Smallest to Largest** or **Sort Largest to Smallest**.

You can also sort the data in a view using the ribbon:

1. On the **View** tab of the ribbon, in the **Data** group, click **Sort**.

2. Choose a criterion you want to sort by, or, if none of the existing options meet your needs, click **Sort By** to create a custom sort order.

3. To create a custom sort order, on the **Sort** dialog box, choose the first field you want to use in the **Sort by** list, and then choose whether you want to sort in **Ascending** or **Descending** order. If you want to refine the sort order using additional fields, choose those fields from the **Then by** lists, and choose orders for those fields, as well.

4. Click **Sort** to sort the view using this custom sort order.

Filtering Data in a View

Sometimes it is more effective to look at a smaller subset of the data in a view. This allows you to narrow your focus on just the view tasks, or on the resources you need to examine. Project 2013 provides two ways to filter data in a view. To filter data that appears in a view, click the arrow on the right side of a column header, click **Filter** in the list that appears, and then click the filter that you want to apply to the column. You can also use the check boxes that appear in the list to select the data you want to appear. You can filter multiple columns in a view using this method.

You can also filter a view using the ribbon, as follows:

1. On the **View** tab of the ribbon, in the **Data** group, choose a filtering option from the **Filter** list.

2. If the filter that you want to apply is not listed, click **More Filters** if you think the filter is already set up. Otherwise, click **New Filter**.

3. To set up a new filter, on the **Filter Definition** dialog box, complete the following:

   - **Name:** Give the filter a name.

   - **Show in menu:** Select this check box to display the filter in the **Filter** list.

   - **Filter:** Complete the first row of the grid to indicate what field you want to filter on, and what you want to look for with that field. Choose the **Field Name**, **Test**, and **Value(s)** for the filter. For example, if I want to create a filter that looks for cost overages, I might choose **Actual Cost** in the **Field Name** column, **is greater than** in the **Test** column, and **[Baseline Cost]** in the **Value(s)** column. You can include multiple rows in the filter to add conditions, and use the **And/Or** column to indicate whether the filter should include all conditions or just select conditions.

4. Click **Apply** to apply the filter to the view, and then click **Save** to save the filter for future use.

5. Click **Clear Filter** in the **Filter** list to remove the filter from the view.

Highlighting Data in a View

When working with a project, it can be helpful to have certain tasks, dates, or other information called out with a visual indicator for easy identification. Project 2013 enables you to set up data highlight filters based on conditions that you define:

1. On the **View** tab of the ribbon, in the **Data** group, choose a highlight filter from the **Highlight** list.

2. If the highlight filter that you want to apply is not listed, click **More Highlight Filters** if you think the filter is already set up. Otherwise, click **New Highlight Filter**.

3. To set up a new highlight filter, on the **Filter Definition** dialog box, complete the following:

    *   **Name:** Give the highlight filter a name.

    *   **Show in menu:** Select this check box to display the filter in the **Highlight** list.

    *   **Filter:** Complete the first row of the grid to indicate what field you want to filter on, and what you want to look for with that field. Choose the **Field Name**, **Test**, and **Value(s)** for the filter. For example, if I want to create a filter that highlights tasks that I haven't baselined, I might choose **Baseline Start** in the **Field Name** column, **equals** in the **Test** column, and type **NA** in the **Value(s)** column. You can include multiple rows in the filter to add conditions, and use the **And/Or** column to indicate whether the filter should include all conditions or just select conditions.

4. Click **Apply** to apply the highlight filter to the view, and then click **Save** to save the filter for future use.

5. Click **Clear Highlight** in the **Highlight** list to remove the filter from the view.

Displaying Two Views at Once

At times, it may be helpful to show more than one view in the Project window at the same time. The viewing area of the Project window can be split into two panes. The top pane can contain the **Timeline** view, or another overall view of your project, such as the **Gantt Chart** view.

When the top pane displays the **Timeline** view, the bottom pane can display any other Project view. With the **Timeline** view in the top pane and the **Gantt Chart** view in the bottom pane, you can drag the highlighted box in the **Timeline** view horizontally to change the focus of the Gantt chart timeline.

To display the **Timeline** view, complete these steps:

1.   On the **View** tab of the ribbon, in the **Split View** group, select the **Timeline** check box.

2.   Click once in the **Timeline** view, and then use the options on the **Format** tab to change the display options and data used in the **Timeline** view.

You can also use combination views to show two views at once with the lower view filtered to show only the data that pertains to the selected items in the upper pane. The Task Form view that we discussed earlier is a perfect example of this arrangement. When you have the **Task Form** visible in the lower portion of the screen, it only shows data for the task you have selected in the upper pane.

A great example of making use of this type of combination view is to have the **Gantt Chart** in the upper part of the screen and the **Task** or **Resource Usage** view in the lower portion. This combination allows you to view your overall project in the upper pane and get the benefits of the Gantt Chart view, while also allowing you to select a task and have the lower pane show you only the details for the selected task. This gives you all the benefits of the **Gantt Chart** view (seeing how tasks are going over time) with the detailed view that the usage views provide, as shown in Figure 2.11.

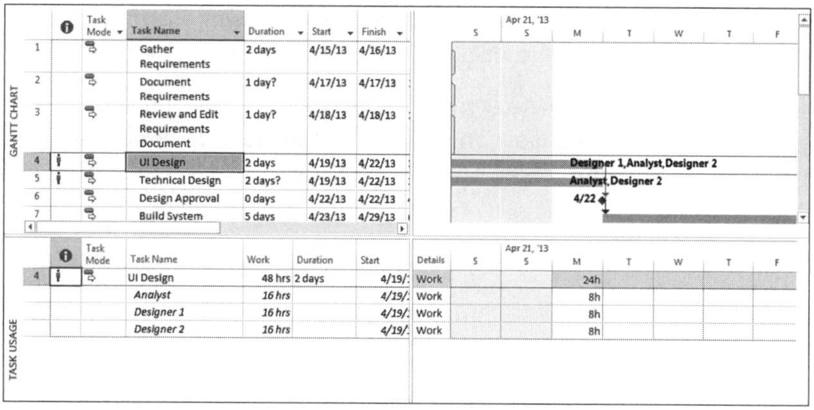

FIGURE 2.11

Display the Gantt Chart view and the Task Usage view at the same time to easily see task assignment details.

To display a detail view in the bottom pane, complete these steps:

1. On the **View** tab of the ribbon, in the **Split View** group, select the **Details** check box.

2. Click **Task Usage** (or the view of your choice) in the **Details** list.

3. To change the display options for either displayed view, click once in the pane that displays the view you want to modify, and then click the **Format** tab.

Using the Timeline

The timeline feature is nothing more than a different view that appears in a special window at the top of another view. It is displayed between the ribbon and the main viewing area in the Project 2013 window. It illustrates your project's tasks on a timeline and can be very helpful in communicating your project data with others.

WHERE'D THE TIMELINE GO?

You can turn the timeline on or off at any time. On the ribbon, click the **View** tab, and then select or clear the **Timeline** box in the **Split View** group to turn the timeline on or off.

If you click within the timeline portion of the window, a **Format** tab specific to the timeline is displayed on the ribbon, in the shaded area labeled **Timeline Tools**.

Adding tasks to the timeline is most easily done in one of the two following ways: Right-clicking a task in a view and selecting **Add task to timeline** from the menu, or clicking the **Existing Tasks** button in the **Insert** group in the **Timeline Tools Format** ribbon tab.

To add several tasks to the timeline at once (see Figure 2.12), complete these steps:

1. On the **Format** tab of the ribbon, in the **Insert** group, click **Existing tasks**.

2. Check the boxes next to the task names you want to add.

3. Click **OK**.

FIGURE 2.12

The Add Tasks to Timeline dialog is a quick way to add several tasks to the timeline simultaneously.

You can use the buttons on the **Format** tab for the timeline to add tasks and milestones to the timeline, change the date formats used for each task on the timeline, and change the text styles used for different elements of the timeline. Tasks can be displayed as bars within the timeline or as callouts above or below the timeline.

After you have the timeline displayed with the information you want to share with others, on the **Format** tab, in the **Copy** group, click **Copy Timeline**, and then choose whether you want to copy it **For E-mail**, **For Presentation**, or **Full Size**. The timeline is copied to your Clipboard, and you can paste it in another application, such as Outlook, Word, or PowerPoint, for sharing with others.

THE ABSOLUTE MINIMUM

The Gantt Chart, Resource Sheet, and the Task and Resource Usage views provide you with 90% of your data viewing needs in Project 2013. With those views as a base, you can filter, group, and sort your task and resource data to fit your specific needs.

IN THIS CHAPTER

- Starting a new blank project
- Starting projects from templates or other file formats
- Setting options for new projects
- Saving your project
- Setting up calendars

STARTING A PROJECT

This chapter covers how to create and save new projects and the basic options that control how your project is scheduled. You will also learn how to set up the calendars that Project 2013 uses to schedule your project work.

The process of creating a project in Project 2013 begins before work is done on any part of a project, before the project schedule is set, and before tasks are even identified. Creating a new project in Project 2013 means simply setting up the framework for the project plan and making some decisions about how the project will be carried out, when people will be working on it, and what factors matter most while work is being done on the project.

More often than not, the building of a project schedule is a team effort, with you as the project manager or scheduler being the person who builds the actual file in Project. Input from your project team is essential at several different points. You may be able to get the list of tasks started by yourself, but to get the complete list of detailed tasks you will likely need help from your team. The same goes for creating the links between the tasks, the duration and work estimates, and maybe even the resource assignments. On some projects, your relationship to the work might allow you to do all of this on your own; even so, make sure that you leave yourself open to the team approach. On larger or more complex projects, assume that this is an iterative and team-based process.

Setting Up a Project

The first step to starting a project in Project 2013 is simply opening up Project 2013 and choosing where to save it.

Creating a New Project

Open Project 2013 and you will see a screen that displays a list of recently accessed files on the left side and then several options for creating a project on the right side. Figure 3.1 shows this screen.

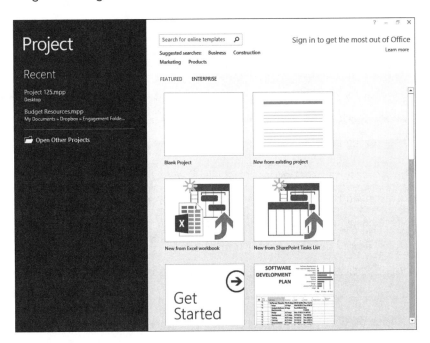

FIGURE 3.1

The Project Open screen provides you quick options for creating new projects or opening existing projects.

NOTE If you are using Project Professional 2013 and want to save your new project to Project Server, be sure that you are connected to your Project Server instance before creating your new project. If you're not sure how to connect to Project Server, contact your organization's site administrator.

To create a new project, complete these steps:

1. After Project is open, click the **File** tab, and then click **New** on the left side of the Project window.

2. Choose how you want to create your new project:

   - **Blank project:** This is just like it sounds. It will create a new blank project. Click this option, and then click **Create** on the right portion of the window to create a new project from scratch.

   - **New from existing project:** This option enables you to use an existing project you have already created as a template to create your new project. Click this option, navigate to where you have the existing project you want to use, and then click **Open**.

   - **New from Excel workbook:** If you have a task list already built in Excel and you want to start your project using that list, this is your option. Click this option, locate and click an Excel workbook, and then click **Open** to create a new project using data stored in the selected workbook. A wizard walks you through the data-import process where you map your task list fields to the correct fields in Project 2013.

   - **New from SharePoint task list:** Here you can use a SharePoint task list as the starting point for your project. Click this option, provide a URL for an existing SharePoint site, choose a task list from that site, and then click **OK** to create a new project using data from that list.

   - **Office.com Templates:** At the top of the New page is a search box where you can search Office.com and its database of templates. There will also be a few commonly used templates listed as links directly on the New page.

Saving a Project

With your new project created, the next step is to decide where you want to save it. If you are using Project Professional 2013 and Project Server, you have several options for saving your project. Professional allows you to save to Project Server 2013, but you can also save your project to SharePoint in a way where it creates a new tasks list. It then keeps your project in sync with the SharePoint list. Project 2013 (both versions) also allows you to save your project as an MPP file directly to a SharePoint document library or to a Windows Live SkyDrive. This section covers the various save options (see Figure 3.2).

Saving your project to a SharePoint document library is the same as saving it to a network drive. Your project is saved as an MPP file. However, syncing your project to a SharePoint site is different. It saves the MPP file to a document library on the SharePoint site, but it also creates a new Tasks List on the site and creates a new task in this list for each task in your project. This tasks list can then be used by you and your team.

FIGURE 3.2

The Save As page provides you easy access to a variety of options for saving your project.

Saving Your Project as an MPP File

1. Click the **File** tab, and then click **Save** on the left side of the Project window.

2. Pick a location where you want to save your project:

   - **Computer:** Click **Computer** to save your project as an MPP file to a location on your local machine or a network drive.

   - **SkyDrive:** Click **SkyDrive** to save your project to a Windows Live SkyDrive location. If this is the first time, you will be prompted to provide your Windows Live account information to access your SkyDrive folders

   - **SharePoint:** To save your project to a SharePoint document library that is not already listed, click **Other Web Locations** and provide the URL to your SharePoint library. If your library is in Office 365, click **Add a Place** and select **Office 365 SharePoint.** If you have already added your SharePoint site previously, it will be listed in the Save page already.

3. Provide a filename and location for your project.

4. Click **Save**.

Syncing Your Project with SharePoint

1. Click the **File** tab, and then click **Save** on the left side of the Project window.

2. Click **Sync with SharePoint**.

3. Either choose to create a new site or select to use an existing site.

4. If you selected to sync with an existing SharePoint site, provide the URL, and then click **Verify Site**. Then provide a tasks list name for your project (see Figure 3.3).

5. If you selected to create a **New SharePoint Site**, provide a name for the site and a URL for the SharePoint server.

6. Click **Save**.

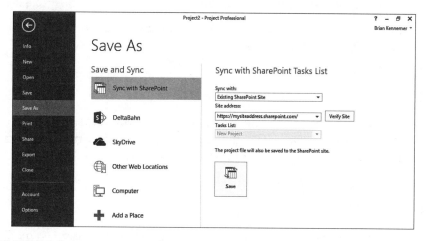

FIGURE 3.3

Syncing your project to a SharePoint tasks list is super easy.

Saving Your Project to Project Server

If you are using Project Professional 2013 and you have connected to your organizational Project Server 2013 server, your Save As page will look slightly different. Instead of the **Sync with SharePoint** option at the top of the page, it will have a **Project Web App** section and the name of your Project Server 2013 account connection, as shown in Figure 3.4.

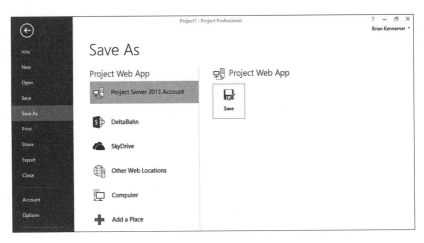

FIGURE 3.4

The Save As page when connected to Project Server 2013 using Project Professional.

1. Click the **File** tab, and then click **Save** on the left side of the Project window.

   By default, the Project Server account you connected to when you opened Project 2013 will be selected.

2. Click **Save**.

3. Enter a name for your project in the **Name** field.

   You have the option of selecting a calendar. If your organization uses departments, you also have the option to select a department. Contact your Project Server administrator for more information.

4. Enter values for the custom fields as needed.

5. Click **Save**.

With your project saved to Project Server, you should consider two more project actions:

- **Publish your project:** Every time you save your project to Project Server, your changes are saved, but they will not be visible to other users of Project Server in reports or in timesheets until you publish your project. To publish the project, click the **File** tab, and then click **Publish**.

- **Check your project in:** When you finish editing and close your project, you are prompted to check in your project. Other users (with the appropriate permissions) can open your project for editing only if you have it checked in. If you do not check the project in, users are blocked from opening your project in Read\Write mode until you have checked it in. To check your project in, click the **File** tab, and then click **Close**. When prompted, click the option to **Check In** the project.

Setting Project Properties and Options

You can set a lot of different options and defaults for your project. And by *a lot*, I mean way too many to cover in a reasonable way when you're just getting started with your project. I do, however, point you to the ones that are the most important and the most commonly used at this point in your project. I then cover other options in later sections of this book.

Setting Project Properties

First, let's look at setting project properties. These properties are a place to store metadata about your project such as title, subject, author, company, keywords, and descriptions of your project. These properties can be useful when searching for your project or for reference purposes when you or someone else revisits this project file months or years from now. To set these properties, complete these steps:

1. Click the **File** tab, and then, with **Info** selected on the left side of the Project window, click **Project Information** on the right side of the window.

2. Click **Advanced Properties**.

3. On the **Summary** tab, provide whatever data is most appropriate in your organization. You can choose to include a **Title**, **Subject**, **Author**, **Manager**, **Company**, and other relevant metadata for your project.

4. On the **Custom** tab, you can include additional project properties by choosing a property **Name**, the data **Type** for the property, and the **Value** for the property. When all three of these fields are completed, click **Add** to add the property to your project.

Setting Project Options

Next, let's look at the default settings and other options you want to use for your project plan. Again, I can't emphasize enough that there are significantly more options than what I cover in this book, but this procedure highlights the most common options that you'll want to set at this point in your planning process:

1. Click the **File** tab, and then click **Options**.

2. Click **Schedule** on the left side of the **Project Options** dialog box.

3. If appropriate, choose the **Calendar options for this project**, including what day the **Week starts on**, which month the **Fiscal year starts in**, what the **Default start time** and **Default end time** are for a typical work day, and how many **Hours per day**, **Hours per week**, and **Days per month** your project's resources typically work. Figure 3.5 shows the **Calendar options for this project** section.

- **Default start and end times:** Set these values to the normal working day that will be in place for your project. The default is 8 a.m. and 5 p.m.

- **Hours per day and Hours per week:** Normally, this should be equal to the number of working hours in the default working day and working week as defined in the project calendar. We revisit this when we talk about working calendars later in this chapter. The default is 8 hours per day and 40 hours per week. If your project team will work 7 hour days 5 days a week, you need to change these to 7 and 35. Then the project calendar should be changed to agree with this working time.

- **Days per month:** This is the average number of working days in a month. The default is 20.

 NOTE The hours per day/month and days per month are really conversion settings that Project uses if you enter certain units of measure. For example, if you entered 1 Month as the duration for a task, Project uses the **Days per month** setting to calculate the number of days for that 1 month of duration. Likewise, if you enter 1 week, Project uses the **Hours per week** and **Hours per day** settings to figure out how many days/hours.

4. In the **Scheduling options for this project** section, shown in Figure 3.5, choose whichever settings are most appropriate for your project. Here are some highlights:

- **New tasks created:** Choose whether you want new tasks in your project to be **Auto Scheduled**, using the Project scheduling engine, or **Manually Scheduled**, using only the dates you enter. You can change this setting for each task individually. What you choose here sets what the default is for each new task in your project. In general, I suggest using **Auto Scheduled** as the default.

- **Duration is entered in:** Choose the time units you want to use, by default, when identifying the length of time you think tasks in your project will take (also known as *duration*). You can choose **Minutes**, **Hours**, **Days**, **Weeks**, or **Months**. You can choose any of these time units at any time when entering task durations. Here, you're setting what the default is for each new task in your project. I suggest keeping the default of **Days** unless your organization is really married to the idea of using another unit.

- **Work is entered in:** Choose the time units you want to use, by default, when entering the work completed on tasks in your project. As with duration, you can choose **Minutes, Hours, Days, Weeks,** or **Months.** Again, here I suggest sticking with the default of **Hours.**

- **Other options:** There are many more options in the **Project Options** dialog, to be sure, and we cover some of them later in this book. At this point, keep the defaults.

5.   Click **OK** to save these settings for your project.

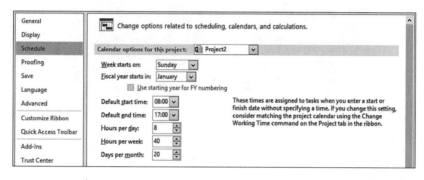

FIGURE 3.5

Set calendar options under Schedule on the Project Options dialog box.

Choosing a Project Start or Finish Date

Within Project 2013, you can schedule a project either from a specified start date forward to the projected finish date or you can schedule it from a specified finish date backward to a projected start date. Most projects are deadline driven, meaning that we know about when we need to have them finished. Because of this, it might seem intuitive for a newcomer to Project 2013 to schedule a project from the finish date. I urge you to resist the temptation to do this with your project. It seems like a great idea in theory, but scheduling a project back from the finish date should be done only by the most advanced of users because of the way it makes the scheduling features of Project react to changes. For the newcomer, all projects should be scheduled from the start date.

To set a start or finish date for your project, complete these steps:

1.   On the **Project** tab of the ribbon, in the **Properties** group, click **Project Information**.

2. Click the **Schedule from** box, and then choose whether you want to schedule your project from the **Project Start Date** or the **Project Finish Date**. Again, I urge you to schedule your project from the **Project Start Date**.

3. Choose a project **Start date** or **Finish date**, as shown in Figure 3.6.

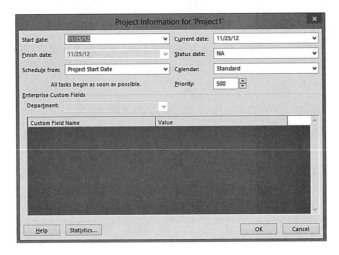

FIGURE 3.6

The Project Information dialog is where you set the Schedule From setting and several other project settings.

4. Click **OK** to save the date you selected.

Setting Up Your Project's Calendars

Project 2013 uses calendars that identify working times to determine when resources in your organization are likely available to work on tasks in your project.

There are four types of calendars:

- **Base calendars:** Project uses base calendars as a starting point for creating the other three types of calendars (project, task, and resource calendars). You can think of them as templates upon which other calendars are based. Use base calendars to enter things like holidays, typical working hours, or other organization-wide calendar items. When you enter a holiday or a change to working times in a base calendar, those changes are automatically reflected in all other calendars that use that base calendar

- **Project calendars:** The project calendar sets the default working times for all tasks in your project. For example, if most of the work on your project happens between 8 a.m. and 5 p.m. Monday through Friday, the out-of-the-box Standard calendar is the best choice for your project calendar.

- **Resource calendars:** Use resource calendars to track the schedules of individual resources. For example, if a resource has a flexible work arrangement and works four 10-hour days instead of five 8-hour days, you can set that resource's calendar to reflect that schedule without changing the overall schedule for all other resources in the organization.

- **Task calendars:** Task calendars are not often used by newcomers to Project, but they can be very powerful. Use task calendars to enter special days specific to individual tasks in your project. For example, if the task must happen over a weekend but your project calendar specifies weekends as nonworking time, you can use a task calendar to call out that weekend as working time for just that task while leaving the rest of the project using the normal project calendar.

NOTE   The following sections talk about base and project calendars. For more information on task and resource calendars, see Chapter 4, "Working with Tasks," and Chapter 5, "Working with Resources."

Modifying an Existing Base Calendar

Project comes with three base calendars already configured:

- **Standard:** 8 a.m. to 5 p.m. weekdays, with a 1-hour lunch break
- **24 Hours:** 8 a.m. to 4 p.m., 4 p.m. to 12 a.m., and 12 a.m. to 8 a.m., continuously, with no breaks
- **Night Shift:** 11 p.m. to 8 a.m. weekdays, with a 1-hour break

You can modify these base calendars to meet your organization's needs.

NOTE   If you are using Project Professional 2013 with Project Server, your Project Server administrator may have the server set up to *not* allow you to specify your own base calendars. Check with your administrator to find out about the calendar settings for your Project Server.

To choose which base calendar you want to modify, complete these steps:

1. On the **Project** tab, in the **Properties** group, click **Change Working Time**.

2. Click the **For calendar** list, and then click the base calendar you want to modify.

3. Review the working times displayed on the right portion of the **Change Working Time** dialog box. Click a day on the calendar to review its working times, as shown in Figure 3.7.

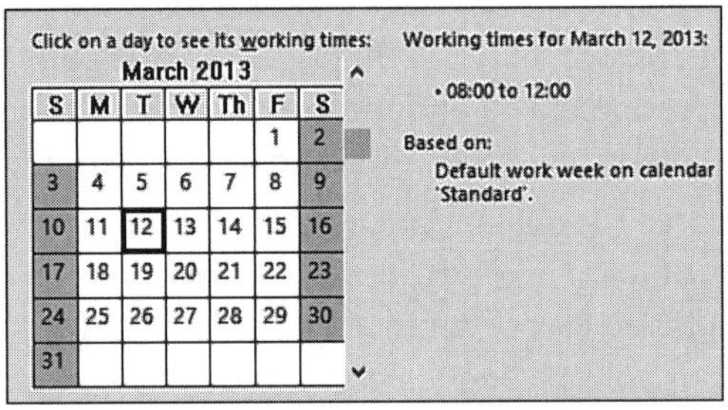

FIGURE 3.7

Working times are displayed for the selected calendar day.

While on the **Change Working Time** dialog box, you can make several different kinds of changes to the selected base calendar.

Changing a Working Day to a Nonworking Day

To change a working day to a nonworking day (for example, to add a company holiday), complete these steps:

1. Click the day of the holiday in the calendar.

2. Type the name of the holiday in the **Name** column on the **Exceptions** tab, and then press **Tab**. By default, the **Start** and **Finish** fields for the exception are set to the days you have selected in the calendar control at the top of the dialog. If those are not the dates you want, you can enter the desired dates.

3. Double-click the holiday, and then click **Nonworking** on the **Details** dialog box.

4. If the holiday is observed on a regular basis, you can set a **Recurrence pattern** and **Range of recurrence**.

5. Click **OK** to add the holiday to the selected base calendar.

Changing a Nonworking Day to a Working Day

To change a nonworking day to a working day (for example, for an event occurring over a weekend), complete these steps:

1. Click the day of the event in the calendar.

2. Type the name of the event in the **Name** column on the **Exceptions** tab, and then press **Tab**. By default, the **Start** and **Finish** fields for the exception are set to the days you have selected in the calendar control at the top of the dialog. If those are not the dates you want, you can enter the desired dates.

3. Double-click the event, and then click **Working times** on the **Details** dialog box.

4. Select the **Working times** radio button at the top of the **Details** dialog.

5. Use the **From** and **To** columns to define the working hours for the event (see Figure 3.8).

6. If the event is scheduled on a regular basis, you can set a **Recurrence pattern** and **Range of recurrence**.

7. Click **OK** to add the event to the selected base calendar.

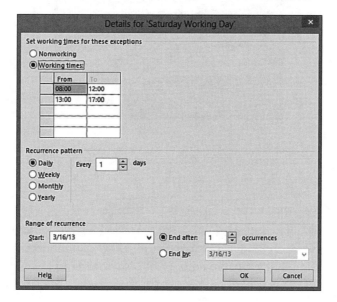

FIGURE 3.8

Set the working times for your new working day.

Changing Default Working Times

To change the default working times for the base calendar, complete these steps:

1. Click the **Work Weeks** tab, and then double-click **[Default]**.

2. Click a day of the week in the **Select day(s)** box, or use **Ctrl-click** or **Shift-click** to select multiple days, and then choose which option you want to use for scheduling on the selected days:

- **Use Project default times for these days:** Click this to use the calendar options from the **Project Options** dialog box to define the working times on the selected days.

- **Set days to nonworking time:** Click this to identify the selected days as planned days off.

- **Set day(s) to these specific working times:** Click this and use the **From** and **To** columns to identify the working times for the selected days.

3. Click **OK** to change the default working times for the selected base calendar.

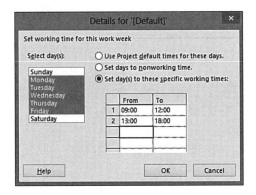

FIGURE 3.9

Change the default working times for your base calendar.

Changing Working Times for a Specific Time Period

You may have specific weeks when the working times need to be different from the default working times. For example, if your organization has a week-long training session that limits the amount of project time to half-days for that week, you can include the schedule changes for that week in the base calendar.

To change the working times for a specific time period in the base calendar, complete these steps:

1. Click the **Work Weeks** tab, and then type a name for the changed period of working time in the **Name** column.

2. Choose the start time for the changed period in the **Start** column, and then choose the finish time in the **Finish** column.

3. Double-click the row you just created to bring up the **Details** dialog box.

4. Click a day of the week in the **Select day(s)** box, or use **Ctrl-click** or **Shift-click** to select multiple days, and then choose which option you want to use for scheduling on the selected days:

- **Use Project default times for these days:** Click this to use the calendar options from the **Project Options** dialog box to define the working times on the selected days.

- **Set days to nonworking time:** Click this to identify the selected days as planned days off.

- **Set day(s) to these specific working times:** Click this and use the **From** and **To** columns to identify the working times for the selected days.

5. Click **OK** to add the changed working times to the selected base calendar.

Creating a New Base Calendar

If none of the default base calendars meet your needs, you can create a new base calendar to use as a starting point for the project, task, and resource calendars.

 NOTE As mentioned previously, if you are using Project 2013 connected to Project Server 2013, your Project Server administrator may have the server configured so that you do not have the ability to add new base calendars.

To create a new base calendar, complete these steps:

1. On the **Project** tab, in the **Properties** group, click **Change Working Time**.

2. Click **Create New Calendar**.

3. Choose how you want to create the calendar:

- **Create a new base calendar:** Click this to create a new calendar from scratch. Working times are set to the calendar options from the **Project Options** dialog box, by default.

- **Make a copy of [existing base] calendar:** Click this to use an existing base calendar as a starting point for your new base calendar. Use the drop-down list to choose which base calendar you want to copy. This option can save you a ton of time if an existing calendar already has most of the settings you need.

4. Type a name for your new base calendar in the **Name** box.

5. Click **OK** to create your new base calendar.

Use the steps in the previous section, "Modify an Existing Base Calendar," to do the following:

- Change a working day to a nonworking day

- Change a nonworking day to a working day

- Change the default working times for the new base calendar

- Change the working times for a specific time period in the new base calendar

Setting Up Your Project's Calendar

When setting up your project's calendar, you need to decide which base calendar you want to use as a starting point. If most of your tasks need to be completed during normal working hours, choose the **Standard** base calendar. If most of your tasks need to be completed during off hours, the **Night Shift** base calendar may make more sense for your project. Or, if your project needs continuous coverage, choose the **24 Hours** base calendar.

 NOTE If you are using Project Professional 2013 with Project Server, the project calendar can be modified only by someone with appropriate permissions. If you need to change the working times in your project, consider modifying the task or resource calendars, as described in Chapters 4 and 5.

Remember that when you set the project calendar you are simply choosing what the default working times will be for tasks and resources in your project. You can modify working times for individual tasks and resources to reflect exceptions to the default hours.

To set your project's calendar, complete these steps:

1. On the **Project** tab of the ribbon, in the **Properties** group, click **Project Information**.

2. Click **Calendar** and choose the base calendar that you want to use for your project.

3. Click **OK**.

4. On the **Project** tab, in the **Properties** group, click **Change Working Time**.

5. Ensure that the base calendar you selected in step 2 is displayed in the **For calendar** list.

6. Review the working times displayed on the right portion of the **Change Working Time** dialog box. Click a day on the calendar to review its working times.

7. Use the steps in the "Modify an Existing Base Calendar" section to do the following:

    - Change a working day to a nonworking day

    - Change a nonworking day to a working day

    - Change the default working times for the project calendar

    - Change the working times for a specific time period in the project calendar

8. Click **OK** to save your changes.

THE ABSOLUTE MINIMUM

Whether you created your project from a blank slate or by using a template, Project 2013 offers several options for scheduling your project. Take some time to understand these options now so that you don't have trouble later on.

IN THIS CHAPTER

- Understand how Project 2013 schedules tasks
- Understand task types and their impact on scheduling
- Entering and editing tasks
- Scheduling tasks to start in a certain order

4

WORKING WITH TASKS

This chapter introduces you to tasks and how they are scheduled, and walks you through task types and how tasks are affected by different task types. It also shows you how to enter task information, set predecessors, and edit task information.

After you have your initial project plan created and saved, the next step is to add tasks to your project to represent the work that needs to be done. Before adding tasks, it's important to understand the different types of tasks that Project 2013 uses. With a basic understanding of task types, you can add tasks to your project, and then set up dependencies between the tasks. Project 2013 also provides a framework for adding work breakdown structure codes to your tasks, if your organization uses them.

How Does Project 2013 Schedule Tasks?

Talk about opening a can of worms! There are a million ways we could tackle this subject, but here's my best shot at summing up how tasks are scheduled in Project 2013. It's important to have a basic understanding of this before you start building your project, so here we go.

Scheduling Methods in Project 2013

Project 2013 has two scheduling methods: automatic and manual. With manual scheduling, the project manager has more direct control of the data for a given task, specifically around the dates, and the Project scheduling engine has less control than if the task were being "automatically" scheduled. As you might imagine, there are pluses and minuses to this approach. The downside to manual scheduling is that you don't get the project management assistance offered by the Project scheduling engine. The scheduling engine is great at enforcing the reality that you have set up around working times, links between tasks, and other factors. A manually scheduled task might make more sense to you because it leaves the dates the way you set them; but what if you forget about a link or some other factor?

With automatic scheduling, the scheduling engine within Project 2013 can make more direct changes to the task data based on factors such as links between tasks, working hours, and resource assignments. If you know a task needs to occur at a certain time, you might find manual scheduling easier to cope with than trying to manipulate other task dates and resource availabilities to get the right dates for the task in question. Automatic scheduling helps ensure that the schedule is keeping with the rules you set up in your options settings. This might make more sense after you have an understanding of automatic scheduling.

Factors the Project Scheduling Engine Considers

When looking at when to schedule a task, the Project scheduling engine takes several things into account:

- **Project start and finish dates:** Depending on how you've decided to schedule your project, tasks will either be scheduled starting with the start date for the project or the finish date for the project. If a task date goes beyond the project start or finish date, a notification appears.

- **Task factors:** The Project scheduling engine takes into account several task factors:

  - **Duration:** This is the amount of time each task is likely to take.

- **Dependencies:** Some task dates may rely on when other tasks start or finish. In Project, these are called *dependencies*.

- **Constraints:** Some tasks may have to start or finish by a certain date. The Project scheduling engine observes these date restrictions.

- **Task types:** Tasks in your project fall under one of three different types, depending on whether time, amount of work, or number of resources is most important. When you have appropriately set the task type, the scheduling engine protects that factor when adjusting the dates for that task.

- **Lag/lead time:** This is the amount of time between the finish of one task and the start of the next or the amount of time that one task needs to overlap another.

- **Resource factors:** The Project scheduling engine takes into account several resource factors:

  - **Work:** This is the amount of time a resource will likely need to finish the task.

  - **Units:** This is a percentage that represents how much of a resource's overall time will be spent on the task.

  - **Calendars:** The Project scheduling engine considers the working and nonworking time identified on the project, task, and resource calendars.

  Chapter 5, "Working with Resources," covers resource factors in more detail.

The Task Inspector included in Project 2013 helps you to find out what factors are affecting a task's start and finish dates. To display the task inspector, on the **Task** tab of the ribbon, in the **Tasks** group, click **Inspect**, and then click **Inspect Task**.

Which Scheduling Method You Should Use

In general, I recommend only using manually scheduled tasks to represent tasks that are happening way out in the future. Because manually scheduled tasks can have partial date information and do not have the same set of calculations performed on them, they can be useful to represent long-range task plans. However, once tasks are coming up in the mid- to near-term, I strongly suggest making sure that they are automatically scheduled so that you can take advantage of the extra dose of reality and fact checking that the scheduling engine brings to your project.

The Project Scheduling Formula

At the core of what the Project 2013 scheduling engine does is the scheduling formula of Duration = Work / Resource Units.

- **Duration:** The number of working time periods between the start and the finish date of a task or assignment.

- **Work:** The number of working periods required to accomplish the task. This is often referred to as the *person-hours* or *man-hours* for the task.

- **Resource units:** The percentage of the resource working day that they will spend working on the task.

Keeping your task data true to this formula is one of the key ways that Project "fact checks" your schedule. When you make a change to a task that changes one of the three elements of the equation, like increasing work or duration, Project makes changes to one of the other elements to keep the equation balanced. A good example of the formula and how it is maintained is a basic 5-day duration task to which you assign a resource. For our example, we will assume that you are working on a project that has the default calendar and scheduling options maintained. Follow along with this example:

1. In the **Gantt Chart** view, type a name for the new task in the first empty row.

2. On the **View** tab of the ribbon, click the **Tables** button and select **Summary**.

3. Enter 5 days in the **Duration** field.

4. Set the **Task Mode** to **Automatic**.

5. On the **Resource** Tab of the ribbon, click the **Assign Resources** button.

6. Type the name of a resource into the **Name** field.

7. Enter 100% in the **Units** field and press **Enter**. Your results should be similar to Figure 4.1.

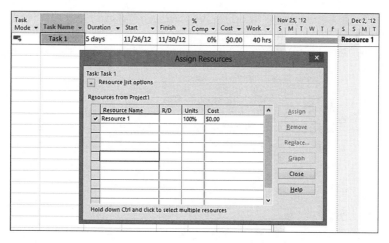

FIGURE 4.1

Assigning a resource at 100% to a 5-day task means 40 hours of work.

Notice that when you assigned a resource at 100% units, Project 2013 put 40 hours into the **Work** field. That is because the calendar and schedule settings say that there are 5 working days between the start date and the finish date of the task and that each day equals 8 hours. Assigning a resource to work 100% of 5 days comes out to 40 hours of work. Now if you change that 100% to 50%, what do you think will happen? If someone works half time on a task that requires 40 hours of work, it will take that person 10 days at 4 hours each day. Try it yourself:

8. In the **Assign Resources** dialog, change the 100% for your resource to 50%. Your results should look like Figure 4.2.

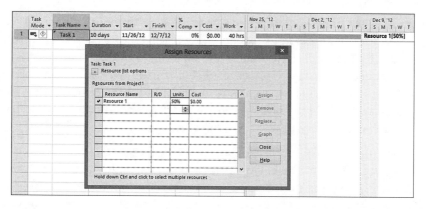

FIGURE 4.2

Reducing the resource units increased the task duration.

This is because Project is keeping its core formula in balance. The change to the **Units** value demanded an adjustment to one of the other elements of the equation. Which element it adjusts depends on the **Task Type** setting of the task.

Understanding Task Types

Task types give you some control over how Project 2013 will keep the scheduling formula in balance. There are three elements to the formula and there are three task types:

- Fixed units
- Fixed work
- Fixed duration

The task types allow you to specify on a task-by-task basis which of the three elements should be "fixed" when an edit is made that triggers the scheduling engine to make an adjustment to keep the scheduling formula in balance.

If a task is set to *fixed units*, Project maintains the resource percentages used for the task. Suppose, for example, that you have a task called "Test product code" and you currently have one person assigned to it at 100% of his time (the task's units). The task is scheduled for 5 days (its duration) and has 40 hours of work. If something changes requiring you to get the task done in 4 days, your options are either to increase the number of people working on the task or to increase the amount of work it's going to take to get to get the job done in less time. When a task is set to the fixed units task type, the number of people assigned to the task can't be adjusted, so Project adjusts the amount of work required for the task.

If a task is set to *fixed work*, Project maintains the amount of work scheduled for the task. Using our previous example of a task with one person assigned at 100% to a task that has a 5-day duration and 40 hours of work, if the duration needs to be reduced to 4 days, Project respects the fixed work task type and maintains the 40 hours of work. Instead, the resource units for the task are increased. You'll either need to allow the one resource to work overtime or assign another resource to help that person get the work done given the shortened duration.

If a task is set to *fixed duration*, Project maintains the length of time you've set aside to complete the task. Going back to our example, let's say that this time you find out that the task is going to require more work than expected. Instead of 40 hours, your resource has reviewed the requirements and estimated that it will take closer to 60 hours to complete the task. Because the task is fixed duration, it now needs to have 60 hours of work done in 5 days. You can either allow the resource to work 20 hours of overtime during those 5 days or you can hire an additional resource to help get the work done.

Table 4.1 shows what changes Project makes, based on task types, for a task that is set to automatic scheduling.

TABLE 4.1 Task Types

Task Type	You Change Units	You Change Work	You Change Duration
Fixed units	Project adjusts duration	Project adjusts duration	Project adjusts work
Fixed work	Project adjusts duration	Project adjusts duration	Project adjusts units
Fixed duration	Project adjusts work	Project adjusts units	Project adjusts work

Fixed Units

Fixed units is the task type to pick if the level of effort on your project is important to you. Suppose, for example, that you assign a resource to a task and you know that you can use that resource for that task only half time. You assign the resource at 50% (units). After your initial planning, you find out that you need to make the task longer, or you discover that the task may take more work than you thought. You don't want Project to change the units, so you choose the fixed units task type. This leaves the resource assigned at 50%, and Project recalculates the work or duration, based on what factor you changed.

Looking at this from a formula perspective, say the original duration of the task is 5 days, the work is initially set to 20 hours, and the units is set to 50%. The formula would look like this: 5d = 20h / 50%. If the task is fixed units, you can't change the 50%.

- **Changed duration:** If the duration is increased to 10 days, Project adjusts the 20 hours of work to maintain a balanced equation: 10d = 40h / 50%. Because the task is set to fixed units, the resource always work at 50%. So, if you increase the duration, the resource works more hours. Project increases the work to 40 hours.

- **Changed work:** If the work is increased to 40 hours, Project adjusts the 5 days of duration, because the resource is able to work at only 50%, or 20 hours per week. It will take the resource 10 days to get 40 hours of work done, working 20 hours per week. This adjustment maintains a balanced equation: 10d = 40h / 50%.

Fixed Work

If a task is set to fixed work, Project maintains the amount of work scheduled for the task. Look again at the previous example: 5d = 20h / 50%.

- **Changed units:** If you need to keep the task set to 20 hours of work, and you find out that your resource is only available at 25% instead of 50%, Project will adjust the duration to 10 days because it will take the resource longer to get the work done if he or she is working fewer hours each week. This maintains a balanced equation: 10d = 20h / 25%.

- **Changed duration:** If you find out that you have 10 days to get the task done, instead of 5, Project will adjust the units to 25% because it will take less of the resource's time each week to get the work done. This maintains a balanced equation: 10d = 20h / 25%.

Fixed Duration

If a task is set to fixed duration, Project maintains the length of time you've set aside to complete the task. Again, return to the example: 5d = 20h / 50%.

- **Changed work:** If the amount of work increases to 40 hours, with the duration fixed at 5 days, Project adjusts the resource units. Instead of 50%, the task now requires 100% to get 40 hours of work done in 5 days. The balanced equation is 5d = 40h / 100%. You can get to 100% by increasing the amount of time the existing resource works in a week or by assigning additional resources to the task.

- **Changed units:** If you find out that the resource assigned to the task is now available at 100% of his or her time, Project adjusts the amount of work for the task to maintain the 5 days of duration: 5d = 40h / 100%. Because the resource is assigned at 100%, he or she can fit in 40 hours of work in 5 days, instead of 20 hours.

Adding Tasks to Your Project

When adding tasks to your project in Project 2013, you can choose to fill out a lot of detail about your tasks upfront or you can enter some basic scheduling information at first and then fill in more details later on down the line.

Adding a New Task

To add a new task to your project, complete these steps:

1. In the **Gantt Chart** view, type a name for the new task in the first empty row of the **Task Name** column.

     NOTE If you want to insert a new task between two existing tasks, right-click a task row and click **Insert Task** to add a new row above the row you right-clicked.

2. Click the **Task Mode** column, and then choose whether you want the task to be **Manually Scheduled** or **Auto Scheduled**.

3. Type the number of days over which you want the task work completed in the **Duration** column. You can also use minutes (m), hours (h), weeks (w), or months (mo) if one of these would be more appropriate for your project.

4. Set the task's **Start** and **Finish** dates:

    -   If you selected **Auto Scheduled** in step 2, the **Start** and **Finish** columns are automatically populated with the appropriate dates based on the project scheduling options you chose when you created the project. I suggest that you *not* edit start or finish dates directly, as doing so sets a constraint on the task that can limit the ability of the scheduling engine to properly adjust your schedule based on changes. Let the links between tasks and the duration of the tasks adjust the start and finish of tasks.

    -   If you selected **Manually Scheduled** in step 2, you can specify a start or finish date, and Project will calculate the other for you.

5. To set additional task details, on the **View** tab of the ribbon, in the **Split View** group, click **Details** to display the **Task Form** view, split with the **Gantt Chart** view, as shown in Figure 4.3.

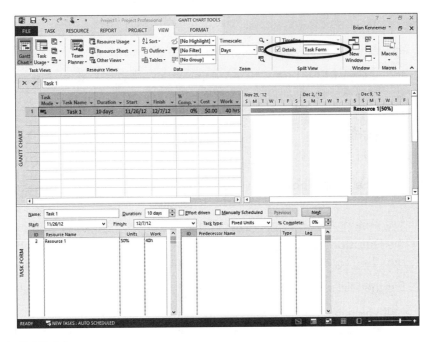

FIGURE 4.3

Click Details on the Task tab to display the Task Details Form view, split with the Gantt Chart view.

6. Use the **Task Details Form** view to set the following:

   • **Task type:** Choose whether the task is **Fixed Duration**, **Fixed Units**, or **Fixed Work**.

   • **Constraint:** By default, this field is set to **As Soon as Possible**, meaning that the task could happen at any appropriate time in the project. Although you can set a different constraint on your task, it is highly suggested that as a newcomer to Project that you leave the default active.

   • **Resource Assignment:** You can create and edit resource assignments in the **Task Form**.

   • **Predecessor Tasks:** The **Task Form** also allows you to specify predecessor tasks for a given task.

7. Click **OK** to save your task settings.

Setting a Task Calendar

A task in your project might sometimes need to use a different schedule from the rest of your project. For example, let's say most of your project is taking place in the United States, so your project's calendar has U.S. federal holidays as nonworking time. However, one task in your project will be completed in another country, by resources in that country. You can set a separate calendar for that task so that the U.S. federal holidays are working days and the holidays observed in that country are nonworking days.

To set a separate calendar for a task, complete these steps:

1. On the **Project** tab of the ribbon, in the **Properties** group, click **Change Working Time**.

2. Click **Create New Calendar**.

3. Choose how you want to create the task's calendar:

   • **Create new base calendar:** Click this to create a new calendar for your task from scratch. By default, working times will be set to the calendar options from the **Project Options** dialog box.

   • **Make a copy of [existing base] calendar:** Click this to use an existing base calendar as a starting point for your task's calendar. Use the drop-down list to choose which base calendar you want to copy.

4. Type a name for your task's calendar in the **Name** box. You might want to use a name that helps to identify this as a calendar that is intended for use on a specific task. This will help to differentiate it from the base calendars for your project.

5. Click **OK** to create your task's calendar.

6. Set the working days, nonworking days, default working times, and working times for specific time periods in your task's calendar. For more information about these procedures, see the corresponding sections in Chapter 3.

7. Now that your new base calendar is set up and saved, double-click the task row in the **Gantt Chart** view.

8. Click the **Advanced** tab, and then choose the calendar you just created from the **Calendar** list.

9. Click **OK** to save the calendar setting.

Indenting and Outdenting Tasks

After you have a list of tasks added to your project, you might find that you want to add some organizational structure to your tasks. You can indent and outdent tasks to add hierarchy to your project. Tasks that have other tasks indented below them are called *summary tasks*. Tasks that are indented below another task are called *subtasks*. Summary tasks roll up data from their subtasks (see Figure 4.4). For example, if a summary task has two subtasks, the summary task takes the earliest start date and the latest finish date from those subtasks.

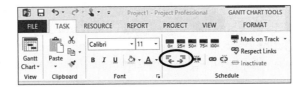

		Task Mode	Task Name	Duration	Start	Finish	Nov 25, '12 S M T W T F S	Dec 2, '12 S M T W
1			◢ Phase 1	7 days	11/26/12	12/4/12		
2			Task A	5 days	11/26/12	11/30/12		
3			Task B	3 days	11/26/12	11/28/12		
4			Task C	7 days	11/26/12	12/4/12		

FIGURE 4.4

Subtasks roll up data to the summary task level.

To indent or outdent a task, click the task in the **Gantt Chart** view to select it, and then, on the **Task** tab of the ribbon, in the **Schedule** group, click **Indent** or **Outdent**, as shown in Figure 4.5.

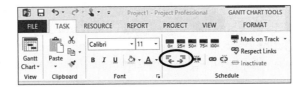

FIGURE 4.5

Use the Indent and Outdent buttons to create hierarchy in your tasks.

 NOTE You can also choose to display the project summary task, which will roll all tasks and summary tasks up to the very top level of the project. To display the project summary task, click the **Gantt Chart Tools | Format** tab on the ribbon and check the **Project Summary Task** check box.

Setting Up Task Dependencies

Some tasks in your project may have certain relationships with other tasks in your project. For example, you might have a task that can't begin until another task has ended. These relationships are called *dependencies*. Project offers four different types of dependencies for your project's tasks:

- **Finish-to-Start (FS) :** An FS dependency is where a second task cannot begin until the first task has ended.

- **Start-to-Start (SS) :** An SS dependency is where a second task cannot begin until the first task has also begun.

- **Finish-to-Finish (FF) :** An FF dependency is where a second task cannot finish until the first task has also finished.

- **Start-to-Finish (SF) :** An SF dependency is where a second task cannot finish until the first task has begun.

Figure 4.6 shows these four types of dependencies.

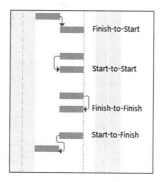

FIGURE 4.6

Project provides four types of dependencies.

Let's walk through an example that uses all four of these types of dependencies. In this example, you are planning to remodel the kitchen and dining area in a home. You use Project to track each of the tasks involved in this process.

Here are the tasks you want to track for the remodel:

- **Rewire Kitchen:** This involves moving outlets, wiring through cabinets for a built-in microwave, and adding an outlet on a kitchen island.

- **Install New Cabinets:** This involves installing new wall cabinets and cabinets to support a new countertop.

- **Paint:** This involves painting both the kitchen and dining areas.
- **Install Counters:** This involves placing a new countertop on top of the new cabinetry.
- **Install New Floors:** This involves placing new flooring in both the kitchen and dining areas.
- **Install New Appliances:** This involves installing several new kitchen appliances.

Each task has some sort of dependency on another task. The Rewire Kitchen task can't be finished until the Install New Cabinets task has started because some of the wiring needs to be done through the new cabinetry (wiring for a built-in microwave and an outlet on the island). This is an SF dependency in Project.

The Paint task has an SS dependency on the Rewire Kitchen task. That is, the painting can't start until the electrician has started the process of rewiring. The electrician needs to have moved openings for outlets and light fixtures, as necessary, before the painters can come in and begin painting the kitchen and dining areas. The electrician doesn't need to be done with all of his work for the remodel before the painters can start, just the portion of work that impacts the painters.

The Install Counters task can't start until the Paint task has finished. By setting up this FS dependency, you avoid getting drips of paint all over the shiny new countertops. This type of dependency is most commonly used in project plans.

The Install New Floors task can't finish until the Paint task has finished. The painters begin by painting the ceiling in both the kitchen and dining areas, then move on to painting the kitchen. After the kitchen is painted, the flooring installers begin their work in the kitchen, while the painters finish painting the dining room. The flooring team can't finish its work until the painters have finished painting the dining room. At that time, the flooring team can finish its work by flooring the dining room. In Project, this is represented as an FF task.

Finally, the Install New Appliances task can't start until the Install New Floors task has finished. This is another FS dependency.

Project represents these task dependencies on the Gantt chart using arrows between the tasks. Figure 4.7 shows how our example might look if we entered it into Project and set up the dependencies.

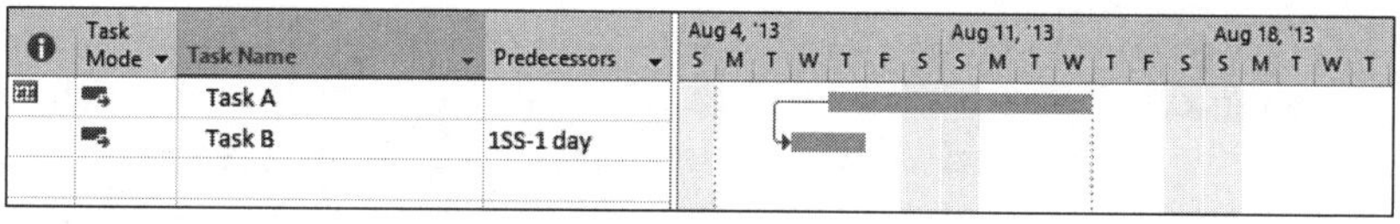

FIGURE 4.7

An example of dependencies within our kitchen remodeling project.

Adding Dependencies Between Tasks

In Project, dependencies between tasks are recorded in the row for the second task in the dependency. For example, if you are creating a dependency where Task B can't start until Task A has finished (an FS dependency), you record the dependency in the row for Task B. When you record the dependency, you indicate the task's *predecessor*.

To set up a dependency between two tasks, complete these steps:

1. In the **Gantt Chart** view, click the task you want to be the predecessor in the link you will create.

2. While holding down the **Ctrl** key on your keyboard, click the task you want to be the successor in the link.

3. On the **Task** tab of the ribbon, in the **Schedule** group, click the **Link the selected tasks** button or press **Ctrl+F2**. This creates an FS link between the first task you had selected and the second task.

4. In the **Predecessors** field, you will see the link in the second task. For example, if you selected 'Task A' with ID 1 first and then 'Task B' with ID 2 first, you will see **1FS** in the **Predecessors** field of Task B. To change the type of link, you can simply edit the two letter code:

   - **Start-to-Start:** To indicate that Task B can start only after Task A has started, change **1FS** to **1SS** in the **Predecessors** column for Task B.

   - **Finish-to-Finish:** To indicate that Task B can finish only after Task A has finished, change **1FS** to **1FF** in the **Predecessors** column for Task B.

   - **Start-to-Finish:** To indicate that Task B can finish only after Task A has started, change **1FS** to **1SF** in the **Predecessors** column for Task B.

5. If one of your tasks needs to overlap another (known as *lead time*), or needs to fall behind another (known as *lag time*) by a certain amount, type this in the **Predecessors** column, as well:

   - **Overlap two tasks:** To overlap two tasks, type a negative duration, or percentage, after the task ID number and dependency type in the

Predecessors column, as shown in the examples in Figure 4.7. For our example, if you want Task B to start 1 day before Task A is scheduled to start, type **1SS-1d** in the **Predecessors** column for Task B.

6. You can also edit the links between tasks by double-clicking the link line between the task bars on the **Gantt Chart** view. This brings up the **Task Dependency** dialog box shown in Figure 4.8, where you can easily edit the dependency type and lag.

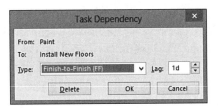

FIGURE 4.8

The Task Dependency dialog box.

Creating a Work Breakdown Structure

Some organizations require the use of a work breakdown structure to align project tasks with things like accounting systems or business strategies. A work breakdown structure, or WBS, is really just an elaborate outline, providing each task with a WBS code that identifies where it falls within your project plan.

Suppose, for example, that you have a project with the task structure shown in Table 4.2.

TABLE 4.2 Task Structure Example

Task
Design Phase
Identify requirements
Conduct survey
Prioritize results
Write specification document
Develop Phase
Code product
Write code
Test code

In a WBS code, each indent level in your task structure is given a set of letters, numbers, or characters that you define. For example, the phases in our example may be given a set of characters, the tasks may be given a number, and the sub-tasks may be given a lowercase letter. In Project, you can also assign a prefix for the code to indicate the task's project. If we use the combination of characters, numbers, and letters just described, with a prefix of EX_ to indicate that this is an example project, the WBS codes might be assigned as shown in Table 4.3.

TABLE 4.3   WBS Codes

Task	WBS Code
Design Phase	EX_Design
Identify requirements	EX_Design_1
Conduct survey	EX_Design_1.a
Prioritize results	EX_Design_1.b
Write specification document	EX_Design_2
Develop Phase	EX_Develop
Code product	EX_Develop_1
Write code	EX_Develop_1.a
Test code	EX_Develop_1.b

Project also includes automatic outline numbers that simply use increasing numbers, separated by periods, to indicate where a task falls within a project. Table 4.4 shows our example tasks, WBS codes, and their corresponding Project outline numbers.

TABLE 4.4   Outline Numbers

Task	WBS Code	Outline Number
Design Phase	EX_Design	1
Identify requirements	EX_Design_1	1.1
Conduct survey	EX_Design_1.a	1.1.1
Prioritize results	EX_Design_1.b	1.1.2
Write specification document	EX_Design_2	1.2
Develop Phase	EX_Develop	2
Code product	EX_Develop_1	2.1
Write code	EX_Develop_1.a	2.1.1
Test code	EX_Develop_1.b	2.1.2

To display outline numbers for your project, with the **Gantt Chart** view displayed, click the **Format** tab on the ribbon, and then select the **Outline Number** check box, in the **Show/Hide** group. The outline numbers appear to the left of each task's name.

CONFUSED ABOUT WHEN TO USE WHICH?

This really depends on your organization. If you're just trying to identify where a task falls in your project, outline numbers may be enough. However, if you're using the numbers to sync with another system, or to communicate with others about your project, WBS codes provide a richer and more descriptive way of outlining your project's tasks.

Setting Your Project's WBS Code Structure

You can set your project's WBS code structure at the beginning of your project, before you have tasks added, if you know enough about how many levels of tasks you might use and what information the code needs to capture. You might, however, have an easier time building out your WBS code structure after you know what your project's tasks really look like.

To set up a WBS code structure for your project, complete these steps:

1. On the **Project** tab of the ribbon, in the **Properties** group, click **WBS**, and then click **Define Code**.

2. If you want to use a prefix to identify which project the tasks belong to, type a prefix in the **Project Code Prefix** box (see Figure 4.9).

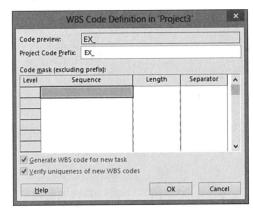

FIGURE 4.9

Use the Project Code Prefix box to include text before the ordered portion of the WBS codec.

NOTE As you build out your WBS code structure, the **Code preview** box shows an example of what your code will look like for a task at the lowest level in your project.

3. Use the columns and rows in the **Code mask** table to build out your WBS code structure (see Figure 4.10). Each row represents an indent level for tasks in your project:

    • **Sequence:** Choose whether you want to use **Numbers, Uppercase Letters, Lowercase Letters,** or **Characters**.

     NOTE If you choose to use **Characters,** the **Code preview** box shows an asterisk (*) as a placeholder for the characters, and you can type the characters in the WBS field for your project once you have your code structure set up.

    • **Length:** Choose the number of characters you want to use for this part of your WBS code. Consider that if you choose one character and if the number of tasks at this level goes beyond nine a WBS code will not be assigned and you'll receive an error message. Also consider that if you choose two or more characters, single-digit numbers will begin with a 0 (for example, 01, 02, 03, and so on). If you want to avoid both of these circumstances, leave it set to **Any**.

    • **Separator:** Choose a character to separate this part of your WBS code from the next part. You can choose one of the built-in separators (period, hyphen, plus sign, or slash) or type one of your own.

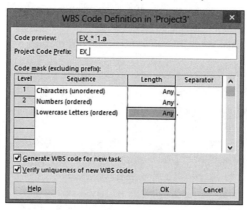

FIGURE 4.10

Use the Code mask table to define your WBS code.

4. Select the **Generate WBS code for new task** check box if you want to automatically create a WBS code for each task you add to your project.

5. Select the **Verify uniqueness of new WBS codes** check box if you want each WBS code to be unique. This can be helpful if you have used the **Characters** option in the **Sequence** column.

6. Click **OK** to save your WBS code structure.

After you have your WBS code structure set up, the next step is to display the WBS code in the **Gantt Chart** view so that you can see the fruits of your labor (see Figure 4.11).

To display the WBS column, complete these steps:

1. With the **Gantt Chart** view displayed, right-click the column that you want to appear to the right of the **WBS** column.

2. Click **Insert Column**, and then scroll down and click **WBS** from the menu that appears.

3. Now for the Design Phase and Develop Phase tasks, replace the * with **Design** and **Develop**, and Project will roll this change down to the tasks below them in the WBS.

Task Name	WBS	Outline Number
▲ Design Phase	EX_Design	1
▲ Identify Requirements	EX_Design_1	1.1
Conduct Survey	EX_Design_1.a	1.1.1
Prioritize results	EX_Design_1.b	1.1.2
Write Specification	EX_Design_2	1.2
▲ Develop Phase	EX_Develop	2
▲ Code Product	EX_Develop_1	2.1
Write Code	EX_Develop_1.a	2.1.1
Test Code	EX_Develop_1.b	2.1.2

FIGURE 4.11

The WBS field displays your defined WBS code information.

THE ABSOLUTE MINIMUM

The task type is a very important setting for your project tasks. After you start editing your tasks (for rescheduling or when you input progress), you MUST understand task types, or else Project 2013 will do things that will confuse you. Create a test project and play with various task types to see how edits affect the task types differently. If you take nothing else from this chapter, make it an understanding of how task types affect the scheduling of your tasks.

IN THIS CHAPTER

- Understand how to add resources to your project
- Understand resource properties and settings
- Understand how to assign resources to tasks
- Understand editing assignments and reassigning tasks

5

WORKING WITH RESOURCES

This chapter shows you how resources work and how to create and edit them. It shows you how to assign resources to tasks and how to fine-tune those assignments so they match how the work is done on your project. This chapter also shows you how to reassign work from one resource to another.

In Project, the people, things, and money necessary to get the tasks in your project done are called *resources*. By adding resources to your project, you make them available to assign to tasks within your project. Resources can have calendars that are unique to them and can be assigned specific cost information.

Understanding Resource Types and Other Factors

Project supports three different types of resources:

- *Work resources* are the people and equipment that will do the work to complete tasks in your project. For example, a developer for your product is a work resource, and the server he uses to check in code is also a work resource.

- *Material resources* are the things that the work resources will need to complete tasks in your project. For example, if one of the work resources for your project is a plotter, you may also want to include material resources for paper and toner. Or, if you're planning a construction project, you may want to include cement, rebar, lumber, and other supplies for your project as material resources.

- *Cost resources* are the fees associated with getting tasks in your project done that aren't associated with the amount of work put into a project or how long the project lasts. For example, if a task in your project requires a business trip, you include the airfare and hotel charges as cost resources.

 NOTE Cost resources are different from the costs incurred by work resources doing work on your project and from the costs incurred as you use material resources (supplies) to get work done. For more information on costs in your project, see Chapter 6, "Accounting for Project Costs."

In addition to these three types of resources, you want to keep a few other considerations in mind when planning your project:

- **Will other projects use the same resources as my project?** If the resources you'll be using in your project can also be used in other projects in your organization, and if you are running Project Professional 2013 with Project Server, you can choose to make resources in your project *enterprise resources* or to assign enterprise resources to your project. An enterprise resource is a resource that is included in a list of all resources in your organization (the *enterprise resource pool*). By assigning resources from the enterprise resource pool, you are able to account for work that your resources are doing on other projects, not just your own. This helps track resource availability and enables you to more accurately plan your project within the broader scope of your organization.

- **Do I know exactly who/what will be working on my project?** If you know that you'll need a specific kind of resource on your project, such as a developer or a roofer, but you're not sure exactly who or what will be doing the work (that is, you don't know which person or which server), you can use *generic resources* to plan your project. By assigning generic resources, you can identify just how many people or things your project will need, and then you can substitute them later for the specific people, equipment, or other resources that will be doing the work you have laid out in your project plan.

Adding Resources to Your Project

The process for adding a resource to your project differs depending on whether you're adding a resource used only in your project (a local resource) or an enterprise resource available for assignment throughout your organization (Project Professional only).

To add a local resource to your project, complete these steps:

1. On the **View** tab, in the **Resource Views** group, click **Resource Sheet**.

2. Type the name of your work, material, or cost resource in the **Resource Name** column. If you are adding a generic resource, type a generic label for the resource, such as **Roofer**, **Web Server**, or **Designer**.

3. Choose whether the resource is a **Work**, **Material**, or **Cost** resource using the list in the **Type** column.

4. If you chose **Material** in the **Type** column, type the unit label for the material resource in the **Material Label** column. For example, if you are adding fabric as a material resource, you might choose to type **yards** in the **Material Label** column.

5. If you want the resource to be part of a larger group of resources, such as employees in the same role or in the same department, type the name of the group in the **Group** column.

6. Type the maximum amount of the resource's time that can be spent on the project, as a decimal or percentage of the resource's time, in the **Max Units** column. For example, if a resource is working half-time on your project and half-time on other projects, type **50%** or **.5** in the **Max Units** column for that resource.

 NOTE   If you are adding a generic resource, you can use the **Max Units** column to identify how many of that generic resource you may need on your project. For example, if you know you'll need three full-time developers working on tasks in your project, you can enter **300%** in the **Max Units** column for the **Developer** generic resource.

7. If appropriate, type the cost information for the resource in the following fields:

- **Std Rate:** Type the standard cost rate for the resource (that is, how much the resource is paid for specific time units, such as an hourly, daily, or yearly rate).

- **Ovt Rate:** Type the overtime cost rate for the resource (that is, how much the resource is paid for overtime work in specific time units, such as per minute, per hour, or per day).

- **Cost/Use:** Type a per-use cost for the resource, if applicable. For example, several tasks in your project will use an industrial printer. Each time you use the printer, there is an initial cost per-use fee of $250 on top of the standard daily rate.

- **Accrue at:** Choose when the costs will be accrued for the resource. By default, this is set to **Prorated**, meaning that the costs for this resource are accrued as work is scheduled and actual work is reported on a task. If you choose **Start**, costs for the entire task are accrued at the beginning of a resource's assignment, based on the scheduled work for the task. If you choose **End**, costs for the resource's task assignment are not accrued until the remaining work for the task is set to 0.

- **Base Calendar:** Each resource uses a specific base calendar as the starting point for their working and nonworking times. By default, a new resource uses the Project Calendar as defined in the Project Information dialog box.

8. If you are adding a generic resource, on the **Resource** tab, in the **Properties** group, click **Information**.

9. Select the **Generic** check box, and then click **OK**.

To add an enterprise resource to your project using Project Professional 2013, complete these steps:

1. On the **Resource** tab, in the **Insert** group, click **Add Resources**, and then click **Build Team from Enterprise**.

2. Use the **Existing filters** box to filter the list of enterprise resources.

3. Select the **Available to work** check box to narrow down the list of resources to only those that are available to work a certain number of hours during a specific time range.

4. To find generic resources, click **+** to expand **Customize filters**, and then define a filter:

   • **Field Name:** Generic

   • **Test:** Equals

   • **Values:** Yes

5. Click **Apply Filter** to display only generic resources.

6. When you've decided which enterprise resources you want to add to your project, press **Ctrl** and click each resource in the **Enterprise Resource** column, and then click **Add**.

7. Click **OK** to add the selected resources to your project.

Adjusting Resource Calendars

An individual resource within your project may use a different calendar from the rest of the organization. For example, one of your project's resources may be out on vacation for 2 weeks in the middle of July, or a specific piece of equipment is available for reservation only on Mondays, Tuesdays, and Wednesdays each week. You can set a resource-specific calendar to accurately represent when that resource is able to work on your project.

NOTE Chapter 3, "Starting a Project," covers how to create and edit calendars.

To edit the calendar settings for a specific resource, complete these steps:

1. From the **Resource Sheet**, click the resource you want to edit.

2. On the **Resource** tab of the ribbon in the **Properties** group, click the **Information** button to open the **Resource Information** dialog box.

3. Click the **Change Working Time** button.

4. Make your desired edits to the calendar, as shown in Chapter 3.

5. Click **OK** to save the resource's calendar.

Assigning Resources to Tasks

After you've added resources to your project, the next step is to assign them to tasks within your project.

Assigning a Resource Using the Task Information Dialog Box

You can assign work, material, or cost resources to tasks in your project in a few different ways. The **Task Information** dialog box provides a convenient location to identify details about the resource assignment, including the assignment owner and what percentage of the resource will be used for the task.

To assign a resource to a task in your project, complete these steps:

1. In the **Gantt Chart** view, double-click the row for a task.

2. Click the **Resources** tab on the **Task Information** dialog box.

3. Click once in the first available row in the **Resource Name** column, and use the drop-down list to select the resource you're assigning to the task, as shown in Figure 5.1. This list is populated by the resources you have added to your project.

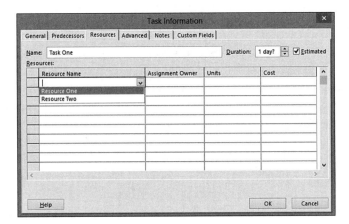

FIGURE 5.1

Click the name of the resource you are assigning in the Resource Name column.

4. The **Assignment Owner** field is used only in Project Professional with Project Server 2013. If your organization is using Project Server 2013 and you want someone other than the named resource you selected in step 3, you can specify that user's name the **Assignment Owner** field. This is a relatively rarely used feature, so be sure to check with your Project Server administrator before using this feature.

5. Type a percentage in the **Units** column that represents how much of the resource's time (or, if you're assigning a material resource, units as identified in the **Material Label** column of the **Resource Sheet** view) will be spent on

this task. For example, if a single resource is working half-time on this task and half-time on other tasks, type **50%** in the **Units** column.

 NOTE   The **Cost** column is automatically populated using the cost information you entered for the resource in the **Resource Sheet** view. To view the populated **Cost** column, click **OK** on the **Task Information** dialog box, and then double-click the task again to reopen it and see the calculated cost.

6. Click **OK** to assign the resource to the task.

Assigning a Work Resource Using the Team Planner View

For work resources in your project, you can use the **Team Planner** view to assign tasks to specific people.

To assign a task to a work resource using the **Team Planner** view, complete these steps:

1. On the **View** tab, in the **Resource Views** group, click **Team Planner**.

2. Click and drag a task listed under **Unassigned Tasks** up to a row in the timescaled portion of the view for one of the work resources listed in the **Resource Name** column. When dragging the task, note that you can also adjust where the task falls horizontally in the timescaled portion of the view. This adjusts the start and finish dates for the task and might result in a change in the constraint for the task. When you are finished, the view looks like Figure 5.2.

3. If you want to add another resource to a task that is already assigned to a work resource in the **Team Planner** view, double-click the task bar to open the **Task Information** dialog box. Use the steps in the previous section, "Assigning a Resource Using the Task Information Dialog Box," to assign an additional resource.

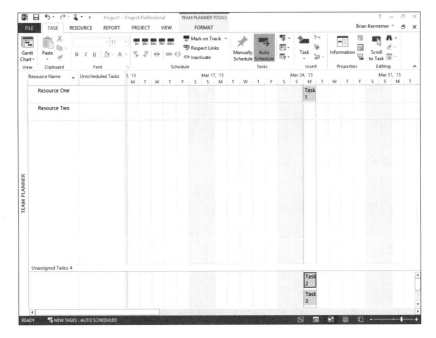

FIGURE 5.2

The Team Planner view shows assignments and unassigned tasks.

Editing an Existing Resource Assignment

If resources in your project have already been assigned to tasks, it's possible that, at some point, you might need to make changes to those resource assignments. This isn't terribly complicated when work hasn't started on a task. Just go back to the **Task Information** dialog box and make the necessary changes. Where this gets more complicated is when a resource has started work on a task and the actual work values have been recorded in the project. You can take a few different approaches in this situation, depending on what changed:

- **If all work assigned to all resources on the task needs to pause and resume at a later time,** you can split the work on the task. This creates a gap between the first part of the task, where the actual work has been recorded, and the next part of the task, where the remaining work is scheduled.

- **If work assigned to one resource on the task needs to pause and resume at a later time,** you can use the **Resource Usage** view to fine-tune the work schedule for that resource.

- **If the remaining work assigned to one resource needs to be reassigned to another resource,** you can use the Task Usage view to move the remaining work to that resource.

Splitting a Task to Create a Gap in Work

By splitting a task, you create a gap between one part of the task and another. This keeps the actual work where it was recorded, but enables you to move the remaining work to a later time within the project schedule. When you split a task, all resource assignments for the task are split. If you just want to create a gap in one resource's schedule for the task, see the next section, "Fine-Tuning a Resource's Work Schedule for a Task."

To split work on a task, complete these steps:

1. In the **Gantt Chart** view, click the **Task** tab, and then, in the **Schedule** group, click **Split Task**, as shown in Figure 5.2. The mouse cursor changes to a vertical line with an arrow pointing to the right.

2. On the Gantt bar for the task that you want to split, click the date when you want to end the work on the first part of the task, and then drag the second part of the task to the date when you want work to resume. Figure 5.3 shows a task that has been split.

FIGURE 5.3

This task has been split into two portions, with a gap in the middle represented by a dotted line.

Fine-Tuning a Resource's Work Schedule for a Task

If a resource assigned to your task needs to put work on the task on hold for some reason (maybe to work on a last-minute, higher-priority task, for example), you can use the **Resource Usage** view to split that resource's work, without splitting the entire task.

To adjust the task work schedule for a single resource, complete these steps:

1. On the **View** tab, in the **Resource Views** group, click **Resource Usage**.

2. On the **Format** tab, in the **Details** group, select the **Work** and **Actual Work** check boxes.

3. On the left portion of the **Resource Usage** view, scroll down to locate the resource that has an assignment you want to adjust, and then look below that resource for the task assignment. Scroll through the time-phased portion of the view, on the right side, to find the dates where work on the task is scheduled. Figure 5.4 shows an assignment with work in the time-phased portion of the view.

	ⓘ	Resource Name ▾	Work ▾	Details	M	T	W	T	F	S
1		⊿ Brian	40 hrs	Work	8h	8h	8h	8h	8h	
				Act. W	8h	8h				
	📊	Task 1	40 hrs	Work	8h	8h	8h	8h	8h	
				Act. W	8h	8h				
				Work						

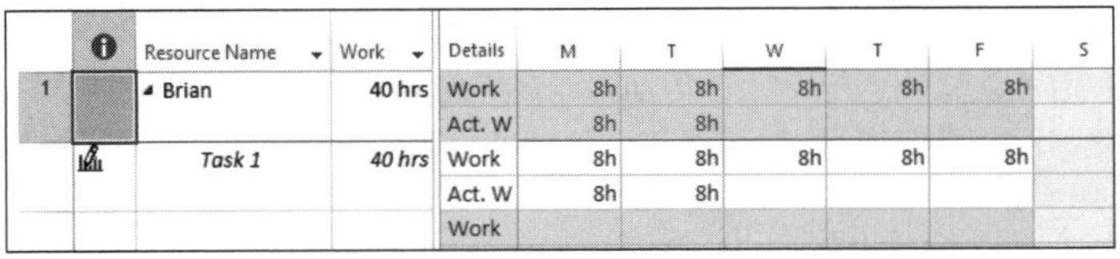

FIGURE 5.4

This assignment has actual work reported on Monday and Tuesday, and scheduled work for Wednesday, Thursday, and Friday.

4. If the resource has recorded **Actual Work** on the task, the best practice is not to modify those hours. The **Work** row for the assignment contains the scheduled work. Any work that is scheduled for after the recorded **Actual Work** is fair game for moving. To move the scheduled work, delete the hours from each day when the resource will not be available, and then retype the hours in the **Work** row for the assignment on the days when the resource can resume working on the task.

Assigning Remaining Work on a Task to Another Resource

If a resource has been working on a task and recording actual work, but then is taken off of the task for some reason (poor performance or a job change, for example), you can move the remaining work to another resource using the **Task Usage** view.

To reassign the remaining work on a task to another resource, complete these steps:

1. In the **Gantt Chart** view select the task that needs to be reassigned.

2. On the **Resource** tab of the ribbon in the **Assignments** group, click the **Assign Resources** button. This opens the **Assign Resources** dialog shown in Figure 5.5.

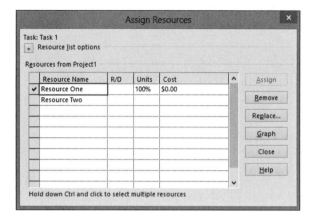

FIGURE 5.5

The Assign Resources dialog box.

3. From the list of resources, select the existing resource you want to replace.

4. Click the **Replace** button.

5. In the new list that appears, select the new resource that will replace the existing resource.

6. Click **OK**.

The existing resource is still assigned to the task, but only for the portion of the task where they had already reported actual work. All remaining work is now assigned to the new resource.

THE ABSOLUTE MINIMUM

Second only to building an accurate work breakdown structure, building your resources and assigning them to tasks is the most important part of building your schedule. Set up your resources to be an accurate model of who and what you will be assigning to your tasks. Make sure your assignments are accurate. Use the tools available to assign and reassign work so that you keep your schedule up to date.

6

IN THIS CHAPTER

- Understanding cost types
- Creating a budget
- Comparing actual cost and work values
- Accounting for overtime

ACCOUNTING FOR PROJECT COSTS

Project costs are calculated using the planned and actual work values for resource assignments in your project. You can also set up budgets within your project using Project 2013 and then compare your budgeted costs with the planned and actual costs. This helps you to track how closely you're sticking to your budget, so that you can determine the next steps, if necessary. You can also plan for and track overtime costs in your project using Project 2013.

Understanding Types of Costs

Project 2013 supports three different types of costs:

- **Rate-based costs**—These costs are incurred by a resource's pay rate (for example, an employee's hourly wages, or a daily rate for a machine rental).

- **Per-use costs**—These are one-time costs that may be incurred each time the resource is used within your project, or within a task in your project. For example, each time you rent a piece of equipment, there is an upfront per-use cost for the rental. It may be possible for a resource to have an associated per-use cost and rate-based cost.

- **Fixed costs**—These costs are associated with tasks, not resources, and they are incurred only once per task. For example, if a task in your project requires you to set up a temporary office in another location, the rent on that office space would be a fixed cost for that task.

These types of costs can be captured using work, material, and cost resources, as discussed in Chapter 5, "Working with Resources." Each resource can have an associated cost, and that cost is incurred when the resource is used within your project.

Note that these cost types are different from cost resources. Cost resources capture fees associated with getting tasks done, such as airfare or lodging. Rate-based, per-use, and fixed costs are associated with work and material resources, and are incurred based on when a resource is assigned to work, and how much work that resource completes.

In addition to these cost types, Project also enables you to do some basic budgeting. You can provide some high-level budget figures and compare the actual costs incurred by tasks in your project with the budgeted costs you outlined during the planning process. The following section walks you through the budgeting process.

Creating a Budget for Your Project

Creating a project budget is a three-step process. First, you create budget resources and assign them to the project summary task, then you identify the budget values for the project (costs or number of hours), and finally, you match up each of your project's resources with a budget type, so you can compare budgeted values with actual values as your project progresses.

Creating and Assigning Budget Resources

The first step to creating a budget for your project is to create resources that represent each budget category in your organization. For example, your organization may have one budget for training costs and another budget for travel costs. To track these budgets in Project 2013, create two separate resources that represent each of these budgets in your project.

To create a budget resource, follow these steps:

1. On the **View** tab, in the **Resource Views** group, click **Resource Sheet**.

2. Type the name of the budget resource in the **Resource Name** column.

TIP   A best practice is to use a naming scheme that identifies the resource as a budget resource. For example, if I am adding a resource for my organization's training budget, I might choose to type **Budget-Training** in the **Resource Name** column.

3. Double-click the name of the budget resource to display the **Resource Information** dialog box.

4. Choose the resource type for the budget resource from the **Type** list.

5. Select the **Budget** check box, as shown in Figure 6.1.

6. Click **OK** to add the budget resource to your project.

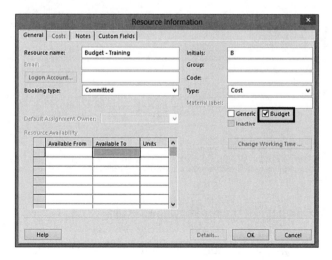

FIGURE 6.1

The Budget check box appears below the Material label field.

After you create the resources, the next step is to assign them to the project summary task.

To assign a budget resource to the project summary task, follow these steps:

1. On the **View** tab, in the **Task Views** group, click **Gantt Chart**.

2. On the Format tab of the ribbon, in the Show/Hide group check the box called Project Summary Task (shown in Figure 6.2).

3. Double-click the first row in the **Gantt Chart** view to display the **Summary Task Information** dialog box for the project summary task.

FIGURE 6.2

The Project Summary Task check box is highlighted.

4. Click the **Resources** tab and then select the budget resource from the drop-down list in the **Resource Name** column, as shown in Figure 6.3.

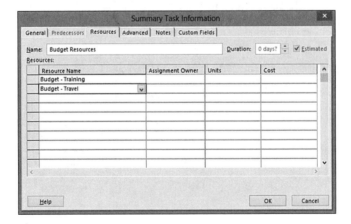

FIGURE 6.3

Assigning the budget resources to the project summary task.

5. Click **OK** to assign the budget resource to the project summary task.

Adding Values to Budget Resources

Right now, you have placeholders in your project for each budget in your organization, but we haven't identified values for those budgets. For example, if you added a resource called "Budget-Training," you've basically said that yes, there is a training budget, but you haven't said how much money there is in that budget. This is the next step in budgeting your project using Project 2013.

Follow these steps to provide values for your budget resources:

1. On the **View** tab, in **Resource Views** group, click **Resource Usage**.

2. Click the arrow on the right side of the **Add New Column** header and then click **Budget Cost**.

3. Click the arrow on the right side of the **Add New Column** header and then click **Budget Work**.

4. Scroll down in the left portion of the **Resource Usage** view to display the budget resources for your project. If your budget is measured as a cost, type the cost value for the budget in the **Budget Cost** column, as shown in Figure 6.4. If your budget is measured as an amount of work, type the work amount in the **Budget Work** column.

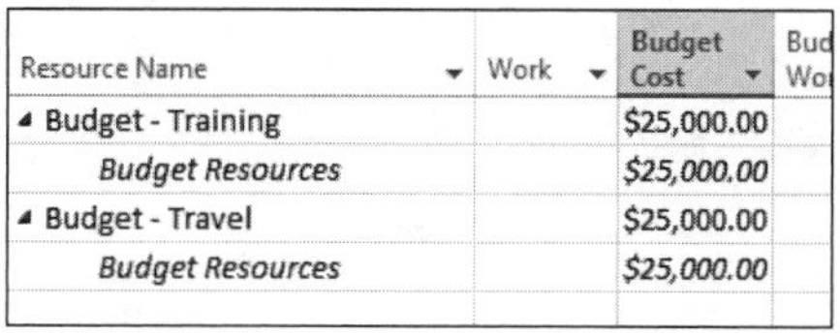

Resource Name	▾	Work	▾	Budget Cost	▾	Budget Work
▴ Budget - Training				$25,000.00		
Budget Resources				$25,000.00		
▴ Budget - Travel				$25,000.00		
Budget Resources				$25,000.00		

FIGURE 6.4

The Budget-Training and Budget-Travel Resources both have budgets on the project called Budget Resources.

Pairing Resources with Budgets

Now that you have your budgets defined for your organization, you can choose to go through each work, material, and cost resource in your project and give each a budget assignment. This step is not necessary for using budget resources, but it enables you to easily compare budgeted values against actual values as your project progresses. This comparison lets you see whether you're overspending, on track, or under-spending.

To match resources with budgets, follow these steps:

1. On the **View** tab, in **Resource Views** group, click **Resource Sheet**.

2. On the **Format** tab, in the **Columns** group, click **Custom Fields**.

3. Make sure that the **Resource** option is selected at the top of the **Custom Fields** dialog box, choose **Text** from the **Type** list, and then click **Text1** to select it.

4. Click **Rename**, type **Budget Assignment** in the **New name for 'Text1'** box, and then click **OK**.

5. Under **Calculation for assignment rows**, select **Roll down unless manually entered**, as shown in Figure 6.5.

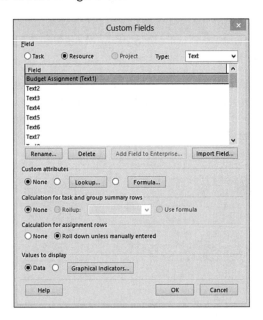

FIGURE 6.5

Select the Roll down unless manually entered option.

6. Click **OK** to finish defining the **Budget Assignment** custom field.

7. In the **Resource Sheet** view, click the arrow on the right side of the **Add New Column** header, and then click **Budget Assignment (Text1)**.

TIP It may help to move the **Budget Assignment** column closer to the **Resource Name** column, so you can see easily which resources you're assigning to which budgets. To move the column after you add it, click the **Budget Assignment** column header once to select it. Now, when you hover over the column header, you see a four-way arrow. Click and drag the column header across the view to a spot closer to the **Resource Name** column.

8. In the **Budget Assignment** column for each resource in the **Resource Sheet** view, type the name of the budget to which you want the resource's actual values to be attributed. For example, if one of the resources in your project is a travel coordinator, you may want to attribute all costs that the travel coordinator incurs on your project to the **Travel** budget. Be sure to type values in the **Budget Assignment** column for each budget resource, as well.

NOTE Be sure to consistently type budget names in the **Budget Assignment** column. That is, be sure you use the same capitalization, spelling, spacing, and punctuation. This helps easily group resources later, when you want to compare actual values with budgeted values.

Comparing Actual Cost and Work Values with the Project Budget

After work on your project has started, and resources have begun recording the actual work, costs, and other values for tasks in your project, you'll likely want to check in on how those actual values are comparing with the budgeted values you identified when you were planning the project. If you've done the work to set up the budget correctly in Project 2013, comparing actual values with budgeted values is relatively easy.

To compare actual values with budgeted values, follow these steps:

1. On the **View** tab, in the **Resource Views** group, click **Resource Usage**.

2. On the **View** tab, in the **Data** group, click **Group by** and then click **New Group By**.

3. Type **Budget Assignment** in the **Name** box.

4. Click **Budget Assignment (Text1)** in the **Field Name** column for the **Group By** row, as shown in Figure 6.6.

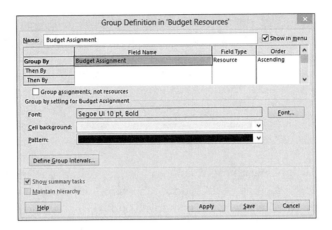

FIGURE 6.6

Creating the Budget Assignment grouping for the Resource Usage view.

5. Click **Apply**.

6. In the **Resource Usage** view, click the arrow on the right side of the **Add New Column** header and then click **Actual Cost**.

7. Click the arrow on the right side of the **Add New Column** header and then click **Actual Work**.

8. Compare the rolled-up values in the **Actual Cost** and **Actual Work** columns for each grouping with the rolled-up values in **Budget Cost** and **Budget Work**.

Accounting for Overtime Spent on Project Tasks

Overtime work isn't defined the same way in every organization. In some organizations, overtime is considered any work totaling more than 40 hours in one week. In other organizations, overtime is considered any work beyond eight hours in one day. Overtime sometimes is calculated on a monthly basis, and other times, extra hours don't count as overtime costs because the resources are salaried. Even within one organization, there may not be a single hard-and-fast rule about overtime. Some resources may be salaried; other resources may record overtime on a daily basis; and others may account for overtime weekly.

Because of this, Project makes no assumptions about overtime. If a resource reports that he or she has worked 10 hours in one day, Project records those 10 hours as regular work. It's up to the project manager to determine whether two of those 10 hours are actually overtime work. After the project manager has manually changed the reported work to eight hours of regular work and two hours of overtime work, the overtime rate for the resource will apply for those two hours, and costs will be accounted for correctly.

Planning for Overtime Work and Costs

If you know that some of the work on your project will be done as overtime work, you can plan for that overtime work before it actually happens. This enables you to more accurately estimate project costs by including overtime rates for resources during the planning process.

Follow these steps to plan for overtime work in Project 2013:

1. On the **View** tab, in the **Task Views** group, click **Task Usage**.

2. On the **View** tab, in the **Data** group, click **Tables** and then click **Work**.

3. On the left portion of the **Task Usage** view, click the **Add New Column** header and then click **Overtime Work**.

4. Type the amount of overtime you want to plan for in the **Overtime Work** column for an italicized resource assignment, as shown in Figure 6.7.

Task Name	Work	Overtime Work
▲ Phase 2	50 hrs	10 hrs
▲ Task 4	50 hrs	10 hrs
Brian	*50 hrs*	*10 hrs*

FIGURE 6.7

Adding planned overtime to a resource assignment.

NOTE Overtime work is considered part of the total work for a resource assignment. If the resource assignment is set to 40 hours of work, and you add 10 hours in the **Overtime Work** column, the **Work** column will stay set to 40 hours. If you meant to indicate that those 10 hours would be in addition to the existing 40 hours, you need to adjust the **Work** column to add the overtime (50 hours of work). Project calculates costs as follows:

(Overtime Work × Overtime Rate) = Overtime Cost

[(Work − Overtime Work) × Standard Rate] + Overtime Cost + Fixed Costs + Costs Per Use = Cost

Recording Actual Overtime Work and Costs

As resources on your project begin work on tasks, their actual work hours will begin rolling in. As the project manager, you'll need to be recording how much of each resource's time is actually overtime.

To add actual overtime work to your project, follow these steps:

1. On the **View** menu, in the **Task Views** group, click **Task Usage**.

2. On the **View** tab, in the **Data** group, click **Tables** and then click **Work**.

3. On the **Format** tab, in the **Details** group, click **Add Details**.

4. In the **Available fields** box, click **Actual Overtime Work** and then press **Ctrl** and click **Actual Work**.

5. Click **Show** to move the selected fields to the **Show these fields** box.

6. Click **Actual Work** in the **Show these fields** box to select it and then click the up arrow button on the right side of the box to move the **Actual Work** field above the **Actual Overtime Work** field.

7. Click **OK** to add these fields to the time-phased (right) portion of the **Task Usage** view.

8. Scroll through the list of tasks and resource assignments to display the resource assignment that has overtime and then click the row header to select the row.

9. On the **View** tab, in the **Zoom** group, click **Zoom Selected Tasks**, as shown in Figure 6.8.

FIGURE 6.8

Click Zoom Selected Tasks in the Zoom group on the View tab.

10. For each resource assignment, look at the **Actual Work** row in the time-phased portion of the view and watch for reported work that exceeds the resource's standard amount of work. For example, look at Figure 6.9. The highlighted resource normally works 8 hour days, and I see 10 hours of actual work reported in one day, so I know that resource has worked some overtime on that day, according to company policy.

Task Name	Work	Overtime Work	Details	F
1 ▲ Phase 2	50 hrs	10 hrs	Work	10h
			Act. Work	10h
			Act. Ovt. Work	2h
2 ▲ Task 4	50 hrs	10 hrs	Work	10h
			Act. Work	10h
			Act. Ovt. Work	2h
Brian	50 hrs	10 hrs	Work	10h
			Act. Work	10h
			Act. Ovt. Work	2h

FIGURE 6.9

This resource normally works 8 hour days, so this 10-hour day includes overtime work.

11. Determine how much of the reported **Actual Work** is overtime work and subtract that from the work total. For example, if my resource reported 10 hours of work, I know that 2 of those hours are overtime, so I subtract 2 from 10 to get 8 hours.

12. Type the new work total, minus the overtime work, in the corresponding cell in the **Actual Work** row.

13. In the corresponding **Actual Overtime Work** row, type the amount of overtime work that the resource reported and then press **Enter**. The **Actual Work** row will be updated to add back the overtime work.

After the actual overtime work has been correctly recorded in your project, the resource's overtime rate will be used to calculate the overtime costs.

THE ABSOLUTE MINIMUM

For many projects managing cost is a key part of the project and schedule management process. For these projects it is important to track your spending against your budgets. Use the budget resource feature of Project 2013 to create budgets against which you can compare your scheduled and actual spending.

IN THIS CHAPTER

- Understanding and using baselines
- Understanding the status update process
- Selecting and using a status update method

7

CAPTURING PROJECT PROGRESS

In this chapter you learn about collecting progress information from your resources and updating your schedule with that information. It also explains several different methods of collecting progress information and explains the relative benefits and drawbacks of each method.

As resources on your project begin work on tasks, they will report their status and actual work hours. If your organization uses Project Professional 2013 with Project Server, some of this reporting is streamlined. However, you can choose to collect progress through more traditional means, such as weekly status reports and team meetings. If you go this route, you'll need to manually enter progress into Project 2013.

Baselining Your Project

After initially setting up your project, you might find it helpful to set a project baseline. A *baseline* is a snapshot of your project data, including dates, durations, work estimates, and cost estimates. By baselining your project, you capture the original state of your project plan so that later, as your project progresses, you can compare what's actually going on in your project with what you had initially planned.

You can also set separate baselines at certain points in your project, such as milestones and stage gates, for example. Project 2013 enables you to set up to 11 different baselines in each project. Saving multiple baselines is one way of saving the state of your schedule at certain key points in your project for later analysis.

You should save your initial baseline just prior to work beginning.

To set a baseline in your project, follow these steps:

1. On the **Project** tab, in the **Schedule** group, click **Set Baseline**, and then click **Set Baseline** on the menu that appears.

2. Click **Set Baseline**, and then choose the baseline number that you want to set from the drop-down list, as shown in Figure 7.1.

FIGURE 7.1

Use the Set Baseline dialog box to choose baselining options.

NOTE A baseline saves an almost complete copy of task schedule data, including work, duration, costs, and dates. If you need to capture only the start and finish dates for the project or the selected tasks, you can use an interim plan rather than a baseline. Click **Set interim plan**, choose which date fields you want to **Copy**, and then, from the **Into** list, choose the interim plan number where you want to capture the selected dates.

3. Under **For**, click **Entire project** if you want to set the baseline for the project, or click **Selected tasks** if you only want to copy the tasks you selected in the **Gantt Chart** view.

4. If you chose **Selected tasks**, under **Roll up baselines** select the appropriate options:

    • **To all summary tasks:** Check this check box if you want the baselined data to be rolled up to the summary task level for all tasks, regardless of whether you selected the summary tasks for baselining.

    • **From subtasks into selected summary task(s):** Check this check box if you only want baseline data to be rolled up to summary tasks that you selected in the **Gantt Chart** view.

5. Click **OK** to set the baseline in your project.

With a baseline set, you can start work in your project, and then use the baseline fields to compare data later in your project's timeline. Baseline fields include the following:

• Baseline Budget Cost

• Baseline Budget Work

• Baseline Cost

• Baseline Deliverable Finish

• Baseline Deliverable Start

• Baseline Duration

• Baseline Estimated Duration

• Baseline Estimated Finish

• Baseline Estimated Start

• Baseline Finish

• Baseline Fixed Cost

- Baseline Fixed Cost Accrual

- Baseline Start

- Baseline Work

- All time-phased data for tasks, resources, and assignments

Gathering Status Updates from Resources

Resources should be periodically reporting their task work and status, either using Project Server or through other means, such as weekly status reports or meetings. If your organization uses Project Professional 2013 with Project Server, resource time and task status are captured by the resource in Project Server and then submitted to an approver who can accept or reject it. Accepted time and status are added to the project, and the actual data within your project is updated.

If your organization does not use Project Server, you need to ask for time and task status regularly and manually add that actual data to your project. Suppose, for example, that you have a task in your project that has a 2-week duration, with two resources assigned at 80 hours each. Those resources provide you with status updates in email, which you manually enter into Project. The resources need to provide you with one of three different "packages" of status information:

- Actual start, percent work complete, and remaining work

- Actual start, actual work, remaining work, and an expected finish date

- Day-by-day timesheet of actual work per day, remaining work, and an expected finish date

The following sections walk you through each of these options, and where to enter the status information in Project, to get an accurate look at how your project is progressing.

Actual Start, Percent Work Complete, Remaining Work

This method of manually recording status is the fastest, but it is also likely the least accurate. With this method, resources provide you with the following:

- **Actual Start:** The date when the resource actually began working on the task

- **Percent (%) Work Complete:** Used to capture approximately how much work has been done on a task, as a percentage

- **Remaining Work:** The estimated amount of work that is left to complete on the task

Using the earlier example, Figure 7.2 shows a task with a 2-week duration (10 days), with two resources assigned at 80 hours each. Notice that the task is scheduled to start on 7/8/13 and finish on 7/19/13.

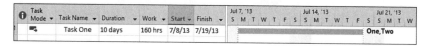

FIGURE 7.2

An example of a 2-week task with two resources assigned.

On 7/12/2013, halfway through the scheduled duration, the two assigned resources provide the following information:

- **Resource 1:** Began work on the task on 7/9/2013, currently about 50% complete, with about 40 more hours of work left to do

- **Resource 2:** Began work on the task on 7/10/2013, currently about 60% complete, with about 20 hours of work left to do

To enter resource status data in Project, you first need to display the corresponding fields, as follows:

1. On the **View** tab, in the **Resource Views** group, click **Resource Usage**.

2. Click the **Add New Column** header, and add the **Actual Start** column. Repeat this to add the **% Work Complete** and **Remaining Work** columns.

With these fields displayed, now you can add the status information you received from the resources assigned to the task. This status information is entered in the assignment row for the task, in the **Resource Usage** view. Assignment rows are indented below each resource's name.

NOTE You can also use the **Task Usage** view to enter assignment data. Add the same fields to the **Task Usage** view, and enter assignment data for each resource indented below the task name.

First, add the information from Resource 1, as shown in Figure 7.3.

	Resource Name	Actual Start	% Work	Work	Remaining Work
1	◢ One	NA	50%	80 hrs	40 hrs
	Task One	7/9/13	50%	80 hrs	40 hrs
2	◢ Two	NA	0%	80 hrs	80 hrs
	Task One	NA	0%	80 hrs	80 hrs

FIGURE 7.3

The Resource Usage view, with status data from Resource 1 added.

To add status data from a resource, follow these steps:

1. On the **View** tab, in the **Resource Views** group, click **Resource Usage**.

2. Enter the date that the resource actually began working on the task in the **Actual Start** column for the task assignment.

3. Type the percentage of completed work that the resource has reported in the **% Work Complete** column. Project calculates the remaining work based on the scheduled work and the percentage you enter here.

4. If the amount of remaining work that Project calculates differs from the remaining work reported by the resource, type the data reported by the resource in the **Remaining Work** column. Notice that the **% Work Complete** column adjusts to show the accurate percentage based on the scheduled work and the remaining work you entered here.

If you go back to the **Gantt Chart** view and take a look, you'll see a progress bar added over the Gantt bar for the task, representing how far along the task is, with just Resource 1's status data added (shown in Figure 7.4).

FIGURE 7.4

The Gantt Chart view after adding status data from Resource 1.

Next, you need to go back to the **Resource Usage** view and add in the status data provided by Resource 2, as shown in Figure 7.5.

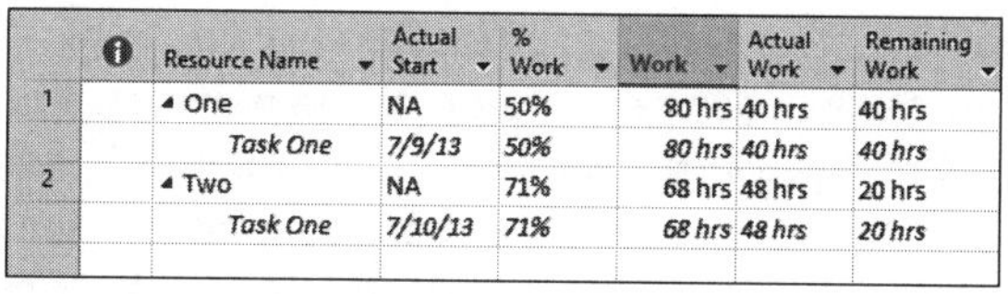

❶	Resource Name ▾	Actual Start ▾	% Work ▾	Work ▾	Actual Work ▾	Remaining Work ▾
1	⊿ One	NA	50%	80 hrs	40 hrs	40 hrs
	Task One	7/9/13	50%	80 hrs	40 hrs	40 hrs
2	⊿ Two	NA	71%	68 hrs	48 hrs	20 hrs
	Task One	7/10/13	71%	68 hrs	48 hrs	20 hrs

FIGURE 7.5

Resource Usage view with status data from Resource 2 added.

Let's take a closer look at the calculations going on here. In the example, Resource 2 has 80 hours of scheduled work. He reports that he is about 60% complete, with about 20 hours of work remaining on the task. When you enter this resource's percent work complete, Project begins by calculating how much **Actual Work** has been completed, using this formula:

$$\text{\% Work Complete} = (\text{Actual Work} / \text{Work}) * 100$$

So, in this example, Project uses the following equation to calculate **Actual Work**:

$$60\% = (\text{Actual Work} / 80h) * 100$$

Begin by dividing both sides of the equation by 100:

$$60\% / 100 = [(\text{Actual Work} / 80h) * 100] / 100$$

This trims down the equation to the following:

$$.6 = \text{Actual Work} / 80h$$

Then multiply both sides by 80 to solve for **Actual Work**:

$$.6 * 80 = (\text{Actual Work} / 80h) * 80$$

This leaves you with the **Actual Work** value:

$$48h = \text{Actual Work}$$

After Project has calculated the **Actual Work**, the next step is to calculate **Remaining Work**, using the following formula:

$$\text{Remaining Work} = \text{Work} - \text{Actual Work}$$

In this example, the following equation is used:

$$\text{Remaining Work} = 80h - 48h$$

The resulting value for the **Remaining Work** column is 32 hours of work remaining on the task.

However, recall that one of the values that the resource provided in his status report was an estimate of the remaining work on the task, and that estimate was

20 hours. At this point, you need to decide which you think is more accurate: the resource's estimate on what percentage of the work is complete or the resource's estimate on how many hours it will take to complete the task. If you think the resource's remaining work estimate is more accurate, enter that in the **Remaining Work** column, and Project will recalculate the **% Work Complete** value using the formulas we just walked through.

Now, let's go back and look at the task in the **Gantt Chart** view with status data from both resources added (shown in Figure 7.6).

	Task Mode	Task Name	Duration	Work	Start	Finish	Jul 7, '13 S M T W T F S	Jul 14, '13 S M T W T F S	Jul 21, '13 S M T W T F S
1		Task One	10 days	148 hrs	7/9/13	7/22/13			One,Two

FIGURE 7.6

Gantt Chart view after adding status data from Resource 2.

 NOTE   You can quickly set tasks to 0%, 25%, 50%, 75%, or 100% complete by selecting a task and then clicking the corresponding buttons on the **Task** tab, in the **Schedule** group. Clicking these buttons sets the **Percent Complete** and **Percent Work Complete** fields to the corresponding value.

After you add the actual start, percent work complete, and remaining work provided by the resources assigned to a task, a best practice is to reevaluate the finish date for the task. The status data you just entered may have pushed the finish date for the task out or perhaps made it possible to shorten the duration and get the task done sooner.

Actual Start, Actual Work, Remaining Work, Expected Finish Date

This method requires more data from the resource but is more accurate than the preceding method. It requires that resources provide you with the following:

- **Actual Start:** The date when the resource actually began working on the task
- **Actual Work:** The number of hours a resource has currently put in on the task
- **Remaining Work:** The estimated amount of work left to complete on the task
- **Expected Finish Date:** The resource's best guess for a date when the task will be completed

You can capture this status information in the **Resource Usage** or **Task Usage** view. The previous section used the **Resource Usage** view, so this section walks through using the **Task Usage** view to enter assignment information.

Returning to the previous example, you are managing a project with a task that has a 10-day duration, with two resources assigned at 80 hours each.

On 7/12/13, halfway through the scheduled duration, the two assigned resources provide the following information:

- **Resource 1:** Began work on the task on 7/8/13, completed 40 hours of work, has about 40 more hours of work left to do, estimated finish of 7/19/13.

- **Resource 2:** Began work on the task on 7/10/13, completed 48 hours of work, has about 20 hours of work left to do, estimated finish of 7/19/13.

To enter resource status data in Project, first you need to display the corresponding fields, as follows:

1. On the **View** tab, in the **Task Views** group, click **Task Usage**.

2. Click the **Add New Column** header, and add the **Actual Start** column. Repeat this to add the **Actual Work**, **Remaining Work**, and **Finish** columns.

With these fields displayed, you can now add the status information you received from the resources assigned to the task. This status information is entered in the assignment row for the task in the **Task Usage** view. Assignment rows are indented below each task's name. If you are using the **Resource Usage** view, assignment rows are indented below each resource's name.

First, add the information from Resource 1, as shown in Figure 7.7.

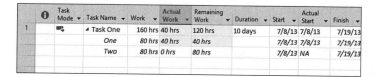

		Task Mode	Task Name	Work	Actual Work	Remaining Work	Duration	Start	Actual Start	Finish
1		🖳	◢ Task One	160 hrs	40 hrs	120 hrs	10 days	7/8/13	7/8/13	7/19/13
			One	80 hrs	40 hrs	40 hrs		7/8/13	7/8/13	7/19/13
			Two	80 hrs	0 hrs	80 hrs		7/8/13	NA	7/19/13

FIGURE 7.7

Task Usage view with status data from Resource 1 added.

To add status data from a resource, follow these steps:

1. On the **View** tab, in the **Task Views** group, click **Task Usage**.

2. Enter the date that the resource actually began working on the task in the **Actual Start** column for the assignment.

3. Type the amount of work that the resource has completed on the task in the **Actual Work** column for the assignment. Project calculates the remaining work based on the scheduled work and the actual work value you enter here.

4. If the amount of remaining work that Project calculated differs from the remaining work reported by the resource, type the data reported by the resource in the **Remaining Work** column.

5. Enter the estimated finish date for the task in the **Finish** column for the assignment, if necessary.

Repeat this to add in the status data provided by Resource 2. Figure 7.8 shows the results in the **Task Usage** view.

ⓘ	Task Mode ▾	Task Name ▾	Work ▾	Actual Work ▾	Remaining Work ▾	Duration ▾	Start ▾	Actual Start ▾	Finish ▾
1	⬛	⊿ Task One	148 hrs	88 hrs	60 hrs	10 days	7/8/13	7/8/13	7/19/13
		One	80 hrs	40 hrs	40 hrs		7/8/13	7/8/13	7/19/13
		Two	68 hrs	48 hrs	20 hrs		7/9/13	7/9/13	7/19/13

FIGURE 7.8

The task with status information from both resources.

Actual Work Per Day, Remaining Work, Expected Finish Date

This method is the most accurate and detailed, but it does require the resources to provide detailed information about their work patterns. It requires that resources provide you with the following:

- **Actual Work Per Day:** A day-by-day breakdown, in the form of a timesheet, for the work that the resource has actually completed on the task (for example, 8 hours on Monday, 7 hours on Tuesday, 9 hours on Wednesday, and so on)

- **Remaining Work:** The estimated amount of work left to be done on the task

- **Expected Finish Date:** The resource's best guess for a date when the task will be completed

 NOTE   Our examples show day-by-day breakdowns, but in reality this could be hours per week rather than hours per day. Although daily records tend to be more accurate if they are updated on a daily basis, it is perfectly acceptable to get weekly totals per task. This requires that the usage view timescale be adjusted to weeks rather than days.

Because the resources are providing a day-by-day account of actual work, they do not need to provide the actual start date separately. The first day of actual work provided in the day-by-day account of work is the actual start date.

You can capture this status information in the **Resource Usage** or **Task Usage** view.

Returning to the previous example, recall that you are managing a project with a task that has a 10-day duration, with two resources assigned at 80 hours each.

On 7/12/13 halfway through the scheduled duration, the two assigned resources provide the following information:

- Resource 1

  - Day-by-day breakdown of work, as detailed in the following table

Monday	Tuesday	Wednesday	Thursday	Friday
8h	8h	8h	8h	8h

  - About 40 more hours of work left to do
  - Estimated finish of 7/19/13
- Resource 2

  - Day-by-day breakdown of work, as detailed in the following table

Monday	Tuesday	Wednesday	Thursday	Friday
0h	12h	12h	12h	12h

  - About 20 hours of work left to do
  - Estimated finish of 7/17/13

To enter resource status data in Project, you first need to set up the **Resource Usage** or **Task Usage** view, as follows:

1. On the **View** tab, in the **Resource Views** group, click **Resource Usage**. Or, if you want to use the **Task Usage** view, on the **View** tab, in the **Task Views** group, click **Task Usage**.

2. Click the **Add New Column** header, and add the **Remaining Work** column. Repeat this to add the **Finish** column.

3. On the **Format** tab, in the **Details** group, check the **Actual Work** check box.

With the **Resource Usage** or **Task Usage** view set up, you can now add the status information you received from the resources assigned to the task. This status information is entered in the corresponding assignment row. In the **Resource Usage** view, assignment rows are indented below each resource's name. In the **Task Usage** view, assignment rows are indented below each task's name.

First, add the information from Resource 1, as shown in Figure 7.9.

	❶	Resource Name	Remaining Work	Finish	Work	Details	Jul 7, '13 S	M	T	W	T	F
1		⊿ One	40 hrs	7/19/13	80 hrs	Work		8h	8h	8h	8h	8h
						Act. W		8h	8h	8h	8h	8h
	📊	Task One	40 hrs	7/19/13	80 hrs	Work		8h	8h	8h	8h	8h
						Act. W		8h	8h	8h	8h	8h
2		⊿ Two	80 hrs	7/19/13	80 hrs	Work		8h	8h	8h	8h	8h
						Act. W						
		Task One	80 hrs	7/19/13	80 hrs	Work		8h	8h	8h	8h	8h
						Act. W						

FIGURE 7.9

Resource Usage View showing Resource One per day updates.

To add status data from a resource, follow these steps:

1. On the **View** tab, in the **Resource Views** group, click **Resource Usage**. Or, if you want to use the **Task Usage** view, on the **View** tab, in the **Task Views** group, click **Task Usage**.

2. Enter the day-by-day hours that the resource spent on the task in the **Actual Work** assignment row of the right, time-phased portion of the view, as shown in Figure 7.9.

3. If the amount of remaining work that Project calculated differs from the remaining work reported by the resource, type the data reported by the resource in the **Remaining Work** column.

4. Enter the estimated finish date for the task in the **Finish** column for the assignment, if necessary.

Repeat this to add in the status data provided by Resource 2, as shown in Figure 7.10.

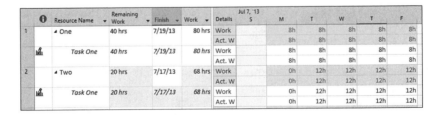

	❶	Resource Name	Remaining Work	Finish	Work	Details	Jul 7, '13 S	M	T	W	T	F
1		⊿ One	40 hrs	7/19/13	80 hrs	Work		8h	8h	8h	8h	8h
						Act. W		8h	8h	8h	8h	8h
	📊	Task One	40 hrs	7/19/13	80 hrs	Work		8h	8h	8h	8h	8h
						Act. W		8h	8h	8h	8h	8h
2		⊿ Two	20 hrs	7/17/13	68 hrs	Work		0h	12h	12h	12h	12h
						Act. W		0h	12h	12h	12h	12h
	📊	Task One	20 hrs	7/17/13	68 hrs	Work		0h	12h	12h	12h	12h
						Act. W		0h	12h	12h	12h	12h

FIGURE 7.10

Usage view showing updates from both resources.

Assessing the Impacts of Updates

As your project is updated with actual data, the dates of other linked tasks in your project will be affected. For example, if Task B cannot start until Task A finishes and Task A finishes late, the start of Task B will be delayed. The series of linked tasks in your project that determine the start and finish dates for your entire project are referred to as the *critical path*. You can view the critical path in Project by using the **Tracking Gantt** view.

To display the critical path in the Gantt view, follow these steps:

1. On the **View** tab, in the **Task Views** group, click Gantt Chart.

2. On the Gantt Chart Tools Format ribbon tab, in the Bar Styles group, check the Critical Tasks box.

Displaying the critical path lets you see whether updates made to your project have changed your project's finish date or other important milestones. If you find that updates have adversely affected the project schedule, you can get more detail about what's driving the dates using the **Task Inspector** pane. Here you can see factors that are driving the schedule for a selected task, such as whether the task is manually or automatically scheduled, what the start/finish dates and actual start/finish dates are, relevant resource information, what constraints are applied, and other factors.

Follow these steps to display the **Task Inspector** pane:

1. On the **Task** tab, in the **Tasks** group, click **Inspect**.

2. Click a task in the currently displayed view to see details about that task in the **Task Inspector** pane. Figure 7.11 shows an example.

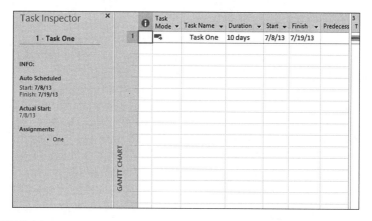

FIGURE 7.11

The Task Inspector gives you details about the factors driving a task's dates.

THE ABSOLUTE MINIMUM

There are several methods for updating progress information into your schedule; some are quick and easy (but low fidelity), and some are more time consuming (but much more detailed and accurate.) The most important decisions to make around status update methods is to pick one that both provides the level of detail you need for your particular project, but that also works for you and your team.

IN THIS CHAPTER

* Reporting on your project
* Sharing project details
* Collaborating on a project

8

SHARING YOUR PROJECT WITH OTHERS

Projects rarely are created and managed by one person in a small room with no outside influence. Project managers have supervisors whom they need to report to about project status, other interested parties who want access to project data, and other project managers who may have some insight into ways to improve project plans. Project 2013 enables reporting, other sharing methods, and a collaboration system to support coordinating project management work with outside demands for project information.

Reporting on Your Project

Project 2013 includes two types of reports:

- **Visual reports:** When you generate a visual report, your project data is exported to Excel or Visio, for a highly illustrated report that takes advantage of PivotTable and PivotChart features.
- **Basic reports:** When you generate a basic report, your project data is formatted into a simple, easy-to-read report within Project 2013.

Figure 8.1 shows an example of a cash flow report generated using visual reports and Figure 8.2 shows the Project Cost Overview report using the new reporting functionality in Project 2013.

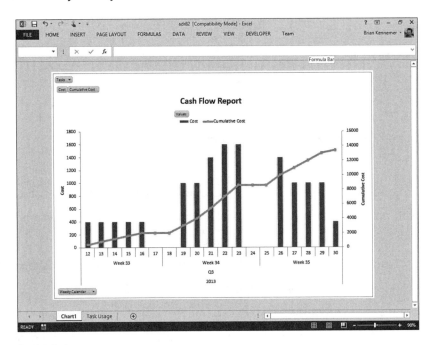

FIGURE 8.1

The Cash Flow Report, a visual report that uses an Excel Pivot chart.

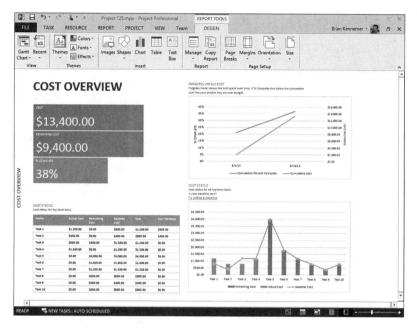

FIGURE 8.2

The Project Cost Overview basic report.

With both visual and basic, you can customize your reports to show the data you need, in the way that makes the most sense for your organization. The process for generating and customizing reports differs based on which kind of report you are using.

Generating and Customizing a Visual Report

Project 2013 comes with the visual report templates shown in Table 8.1.

TABLE 8.1   Available Visual Reports

Excel	Visio
Baseline Cost Report	Baseline Report
Baseline Work Report	Cash Flow Report
Budget Cost Report	Critical Tasks Status Report
Budget Work Report	Resource Availability Report
Cash Flow Report	Resource Status Report
Earned Value Over Time Report	Task Status Report
Resource Cost Summary Report	
Resource Remaining Work Report	
Resource Work Availability Report	
Resource Work Summary Report	

Follow these steps to generate one of these visual reports:

1. On the **Report** tab, in the **Export** group, click **Visual Reports**.

2. Click the name of the report you want to generate.

 NOTE To narrow down the list of reports, you can click each tab on the **Visual Reports—Create Report** dialog box to view only reports that fit each category (such as **Task Usage** or **Resource Summary**, for example). You can also choose to display only reports that open in Excel or only those that open in Visio by selecting or clearing the **Microsoft Excel** and **Microsoft Visio** check boxes. This filters the list of reports by whichever application you select.

3. To choose the amount of usage detail you want to include in the report, select an option from the **Select level of usage data to include in the report** list.

 NOTE A best practice is to leave the usage detail set to the Project default. In most cases, this will be **Weeks**. Including more detail (**Days**, for example) may impact the performance of the report. If the report you are generating doesn't need to include usage data, choose **Years** to get the best level of performance for the report.

4. Click **View** to begin generating the report. Based on your selection, the report will open in Excel or Visio, and you can modify what data is displayed by using the PivotTable or PivotChart features within those applications.

If the default visual report templates included with Project 2013 don't include the right data to meet your needs, you can add or remove data fields to make the report more useful.

To add or remove fields from an existing visual report template, follow these steps:

1. On the **Report** tab, in the **Export** group, click **Visual Reports**.

2. Click the name of the report you want to modify and then click **Edit Template**. The **Visual Reports—Field Picker** dialog box appears, as shown in Figure 8.3.

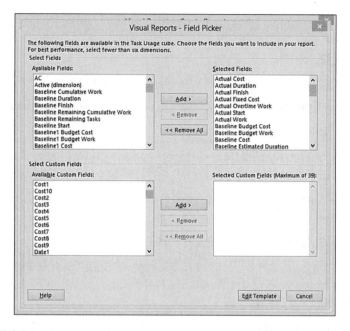

FIGURE 8.3

Use the Visual Reports—Field Picker dialog box to choose fields to include in the selected report.

3. To add a built-in Project field to the report, under **Select Fields**, click the name of the field in the **Available Fields** box, and then click **Add** to move it to the **Selected Fields** box.

4. To remove a built-in Project field from the report, under **Select Fields**, click the name of the field in the **Selected Fields** box, and then click **Remove** to move it to the **Available Fields** box.

5. To add a custom field to the report, under **Select Custom Fields**, click the name of the field in the **Available Custom Fields** box, and then click **Add** to move it to the **Selected Custom Fields** box.

6. To remove a custom field from the report, under **Select Custom Fields**, click the name of the field in the **Selected Custom Fields** box, and then click **Remove** to move it to the **Available Custom Fields** box.

7. Click **Edit Template**, and the template opens in Excel or Visio. Use the features in the selected application to surface the data you added or to rearrange the report to account for the data you removed.

If the existing reports don't come anywhere near meeting your needs, you can create your own report by choosing what format you want to use and what data you want to export.

To create a new visual report template, follow these steps:

1. On the **Report** tab, in the **Export** group, click **Visual Reports**.

2. Click **New Template**.

3. Under **Select Application**, choose whether you want to create the report in Excel or Visio.

4. Under **Select Data Type**, choose a category of usage or summary data that includes the information you want in your report.

5. Under **Select Fields**, click **Field Picker**.

6. To add a built-in Project field to the report, under **Select Fields**, click the name of the field in the **Available Fields** box, and then click **Add** to move it to the **Selected Fields** box.

7. To remove a built-in Project field from the report, under **Select Fields**, click the name of the field in the **Selected Fields** box, and then click **Remove** to move it to the **Available Fields** box.

8. To add a custom field to the report, under **Select Custom Fields**, click the name of the field in the **Available Custom Fields** box, and then click **Add** to move it to the **Selected Custom Fields** box.

9. To remove a custom field from the report, under **Select Custom Fields**, click the name of the field in the **Selected Custom Fields** box, and then click **Remove** to move it to the **Available Custom Fields** box.

10. Click **OK** on the **Visual Reports—Field Picker** dialog box to add the selected fields to the report.

11. Click **OK** on the **Visual Reports—New Template** dialog box to export the data to Excel or Visio and begin designing the visual layout of your report. Use the PivotTable and PivotChart features in those applications to choose how you want to present your project data.

Generating and Customizing a Basic Report

Table 8.2 shows the basic reports included in Project 2013.

TABLE 8.2 Available Basic Reports

Category	Report Name
Dashboard	Burndown
	Cost Overview
	Project Overview
	Upcoming Tasks
	Work Overview
Resources	Overallocated Resources
	Resource Overview
Costs	Cash Flow
	Cost Overruns
	Earned Value Report
	Resource Cost Overview
	Task Cost Overview
In Progress	Critical Tasks
	Late Tasks
	Milestone Report
	Slipping Tasks
Getting Started	Create Reports
	Getting Started with Project
	Organize Tasks
	Share with your Team

Follow these steps to generate and print one of these basic reports:

1. On the **Report** tab, in the **View Reports** group click the category that contains the report you want to generate.

 NOTE Basic reports that you have created are listed under the **Custom** category.

2. Click the name of the report you want to generate, and then click **Select**.

3. Click **Print** to print the selected report.

If the basic reports included with Project 2013 don't contain the information you need and you don't have the option (or don't want) to use visual reports, you can create your own basic report. The steps for creating a custom basic report differ depending on what kind of report you are creating.

To create a custom basic task or resource report, follow these steps:

1. On the **Report** tab, in the **View Reports** group, click **New Report**, and then select the type of report you want to create. In our case, we will pick **Table**.

2. Type a name for your new report. Click **OK**.

3. In the Field List pane on the right side select **Task** or **Resource** to pick whether the table will show task or resource information.

4. In the **Select Field** list check the boxes next to the fields that should show up in your report.

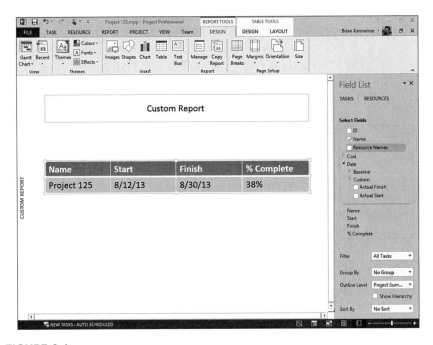

FIGURE 8.4

Creating a basic custom report

5. Select a filter from the **Filter** list to have your report show only certain tasks.

6. Pick a group if you want your report to show the data grouped.

7. Select an outline level. Select **All Subtasks** if you want your report to show lowest level tasks.

8. Pick a sort to control how your report will sort.

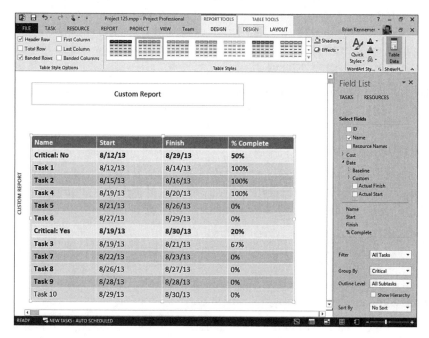

FIGURE 8.5

Custom report showing tasks grouped by the Critical field.

To create a custom chart report, follow these steps:

1. On the **Report** tab, in the **View Reports** group, click **New Report**.

2. Click **Chart** and enter a name for your report. Click **OK**.

3. On the **Report Tools Design** tab on the **Insert** group, click the **Chart** button.

4. Select the type of chart you want to insert. For example, select **Clustered Column**.

5. On the **Field** list, select the fields you want to chart. Type a name for the new report in the **Name** box.

6. As with table reports, select the **Filter**, **Group By**, **Outline Level**, and **Sort** options.

Sharing Data with Others

So, suppose that someone else has requested detailed data about your project. Arguably, the easiest route in this case is to simply send a copy of the file to the other person and have that person open it with Project 2013 on his or her machine. Unfortunately, it's rarely that easy. If the person requesting information doesn't have Project 2013 installed, your options become a little less direct, but not necessarily less detailed.

Depending on what the other person wants to do with the project data, a few different options are available, as covered in the following sections.

Copying the Timeline

The timeline is new to Project 2013 and provides a highly visual way to share project information. After setting up the timeline with the information you want to share, you can easily copy it for use in another application.

 NOTE For more information on using the timeline, see "Using the Timeline" in Chapter 2, "Navigating Project 2013."

Follow these steps to copy the timeline:

1. If the timeline is not currently displayed, on the **View** tab, in the **Split View** group, select the **Timeline** check box, as shown in Figure 8.6.

FIGURE 8.6

The Timeline check box is on the View tab, in the Split View group.

2. Click once in the **Timeline** portion of the Project window to select it.

3. On the **Format** tab, in the **Copy** group, click **Copy Timeline**, and then choose whether you're copying it **For E-mail**, **For Presentation**, or **Full Size**. Project uses different formatting options based on your selection.

With the timeline copied to the Clipboard, open the email message, presentation deck, or other file where you want to include the project information, and then paste the copied timeline. It will be pasted as an image within the email message or file.

Exporting Data to Excel

If the person requesting project data wants to be able to work with the requested data, the right solution might be to export the data as an Excel workbook.

To export project data to Excel, follow these steps:

1. On the **File** tab, click **Save As**.

2. Browse to the location where you want to save the Excel file.

3. Type a name for the file in the **File name** box.

4. Click **Save as type**, and then choose **Excel Workbook**.

 NOTE   If the person requesting project data is using an older version of Excel, choose Excel 97-2003. You can also choose to save the data as tab-delimited text, comma-delimited text (CSV), or XML.

5. Click **Save**.

6. Follow the steps in the Export Wizard to save the project data.

Taking a Picture of Your Project Data

If the person requesting project data just wants to look at the data, without the option of working directly with it, you can copy a picture of your project data and share it by pasting it into another file or email message.

Follow these steps to copy a picture of your project data:

1. Format the data in a view the way you want to share it, and then select the data you want to share. If you want to share all the data in the view, you don't need to select any data; just click once anywhere in the view to select it.

2. On the **Task** tab, in the **Clipboard** group, click the arrow on **Copy**, and then click **Copy Picture**, as shown in Figure 8.7.

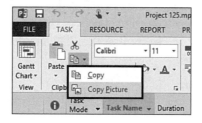

FIGURE 8.7

Click the arrow on the Copy button, and then click Copy Picture.

3. Under **Render image**, choose whether you want to copy the image **For screen**, **For printer**, or **To GIF image file**. If you choose **To GIF image file**, click **Browse** to locate where you want to save the GIF file.

4. Under **Copy**, click **Rows on screen** to copy all the rows displayed on the screen, or click **Selected rows** to copy only the rows you selected before you clicked **Copy Picture**.

5. Under **Timescale**, click **As shown on screen** to use the full timescale currently displayed in the view, or choose **From** and **To** dates to specify a time period to include.

6. Click **OK** to copy a picture of the project data in the view using the options you selected.

Saving the Project as a PDF or XPS File

Another option for viewing project data is to save the project as a PDF or XPS file.

To save the project as a PDF or XPS file, follow these steps:

1. Format the data in a view the way you want to share it, and then on the **File** tab click **Save As**.

2. Browse to the location where you want to save the PDF or XPS file.

3. Type a name for the file in the **File name** box.

4. Click **Save as type**, and then choose **PDF Files** or **XPS Files**.

5. Click **Save**.

6. In the **Document Export Options** dialog box, under **Publish Range**, click **All** to include the entire project or click **From** and specify a date range to only include a certain time period.

7. Under **Include Non-Printing Information**, select or clear the **Document Properties** and **Document Showing Markup** check boxes to choose which options to include.

8. Under **PDF Options**, select or clear the **ISO 19005-1 compliant (PDF/A)** check box to determine whether the PDF should conform to long-term archiving standards.

9. Click **OK** to save the PDF or XPS file.

Collaborating with Others on Your Project

If you are using Project Professional 2013 with Project Server, you can work on a project plan with others who may not have access to your Project Server. By saving the project plan for sharing, you associate the file with its checked-out location in Project Server. You can then send the file around to others, who can use Project Professional 2013 on their own machines to make changes. Then, when the file is returned to you with changes, you can open it up and check it back in to Project Server.

To save a project for sharing with others, follow these steps:

1. With Project Professional 2013 opened and connected to Project Server, click the **File** tab, and then click **Open**.

2. Click **Retrieve the list of all projects from Project Server**, and then double-click the name of the file you want to share with others.

3. On the **File** tab, click **Save Project as File**.

4. Click **Save for Sharing**, and then click **Save As**.

5. Type a name for the project file in the **File name** box. A best practice here is to use the same name as the Project Server filename.

6. Locate where you want to save the file locally, and then click **Save**.

With the file saved locally, you can attach it to email or place it on a network share to enable others to open it. Other people opening this file must also have Project Professional 2013. Although the file is saved locally, it remains checked out from Project Server. When changes are made to the file, you can check it back in to Project Server.

Follow these steps to check the file back in to Project Server, with changes:

1. With Project Professional 2013 opened and connected to the same Project Server on which the project is checked out, click the **File** tab, and then click **Open**.

2. Locate the changed shared file, and then click **Open**.

3. On the **File** tab, click **Save As**.

4. Click the name of the file in the **Save to Project Server** box.

5. Click **Save** to replace the file on the server with the file you were sharing.

THE ABSOLUTE MINIMUM

Sharing your project schedule information with other people is a key part of managing a project. Project 2013 provides you with many ways to create reports or outputs of various types. The key is to figure out what the user of your output really needs to do with that information and pick a layout and format that will best serve their need.

IN THIS CHAPTER

- Creating custom rields
- Customizing tables
- Creating new views

9

CUSTOMIZING PROJECT 2013

This chapter shows you how to create custom fields to capture task and resource data specific to your organization or project. It also shows you how to create your own tables and views to better display the data you need to see when managing your project.

You can customize views in Project 2013 in many ways to meet your needs. Among the more common customizations are custom fields, custom tables, and custom views. By customizing these three elements, you can capture exactly the information you need, and then display it in just the way you want using the framework provided by Project 2013.

Creating Custom Fields

You can use custom fields to add information to your project that is not captured using the default fields that come with Project 2013. That information might be specific to your project, your team, or your organization. Commonly added custom fields include the following:

- **Location:** A field to track the geographic location where a task will take place

- **Phase:** A field to align a task with a certain phase or stage in a lifecycle

- **Owner:** A field to call out a person that owns the task that is other than the project manager or the resource

- **Status:** A field with a custom formula to calculate the status of the task based on current dates compared to baselines

To create a custom field in your project, follow these steps:

1. On the **Project** tab, in the **Properties** group, click **Custom Fields**.

2. Choose whether you are customizing a **Task**, **Resource**, or **Project** field, as shown in Figure 9.1.

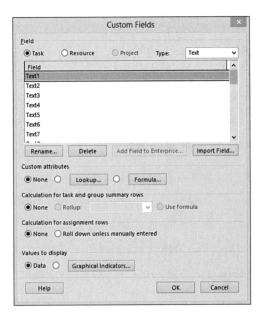

FIGURE 9.1

Choose from Task, Resource, or Project, in the highlighted portion of the Custom Fields dialog box.

NOTE You will find project-level custom fields available only when connected to Project Server 2013.

3. In the **Type** list, click the type of data you plan to enter in the field you are customizing.

4. In the **Field** box, click the name of the field you are customizing. If the field has a friendly name followed by the original (generic) name in parentheses, it is most likely already being used.

5. Click **Rename**, type a new friendly name for the field in the **New name for** box, and then click **OK**.

6. Under **Custom Attributes**, if you just want to be able to enter data in the field, leave it set to **None**. However, if you want to control the data, choose one of the following options:

   • **Lookup:** If you want to choose a value from a list, click **Lookup**, type each of the list values in the **Value** column, choose any other options that may make sense for your list, and then click **Close**.

   • **Formula:** If you want to calculate the value in the field using dates or other project data, click **Formula**.

    NOTE Office.com has a great resource to help you build your own formulas. "Project functions for custom fields" is available at http://office.microsoft.com/en-us/project-help/project-functions-for-custom-fields-HA102749085.aspx. It provides a number of functions (including descriptions and examples) that you can use within formulas for custom fields in Project 2013.

7. Under **Calculation for task and group summary rows**, choose one of the following options:

   • **None:** Click **None** if you don't want the field rolled up to the task and group summary levels. If the field is a Text type, None will be the only option available.

   • **Rollup:** Click **Rollup** and choose how you want the rollup calculated if you want the field values summarized at the task and group summary levels.

   • **Use formula:** Click **Use formula** if you selected **Formula** under **Custom attributes** and you want to use that formula for the rollup values for the field you're customizing.

8. Under **Calculation for assignment rows**, click **None** if you do not want the values in this custom field to be spread across assignments, or click **Roll down**

unless manually entered if you want the values spread evenly across each assignment. If you choose **Roll down unless manually entered**, the values entered for a task or resource will be entered into the assignment level, but you'll still be able to manually enter data.

9. Under **Values to display**, click **Data** to display the data as is, or click **Graphical Indicators** to display an icon based on the data entered in the field. For example, you can assign red, yellow, and green icons to different status descriptors to provide a visual health indicator.

10. Click **OK** to save your custom field.

After customizing a field, you can add it as a column in a view.

Adding and Removing Columns in a View

The process of adding and removing columns in views in Project 2013 is incredibly easy. However, the concept behind what happens can sometimes prove confusing. So, examining how to add and remove columns, let's talk a bit about what's going on behind the scenes.

Remember that behind the interface of Project 2013 there's a database. When you use Project to add information about your project, that information makes its way into that database. Back in the Project interface, we use views to look at the data in that database. Views are set up to slice and dice that data in a way that helps us make sense of it. Columns are just parts of views. They're a way of surfacing specific parts of the database into the interface.

The confusion around this often comes when you go to remove a column from a view. Suppose, for instance, that you've had a column in a view for a long time and that data has been added to the column. You decide you no longer need to see that data, so you hide the column in the view. Then later, you decide you want to use that column for another purpose, so you add it again, and lo and behold your data is still in there. This sometimes comes as a rude surprise to some Project users who thought that by hiding the column the data would go away.

When you hide a column, that's really all you're doing: hiding *not* deleting. You're taking that way of viewing information in the database out of a view. Imagine if you were simply trying to change which view surfaced the information. Let's say you had a column of information in one view, and after you had been using it for a while you realized it would be better suited for another view. If you had to re-create the column with its data in another view, it could really become quite an effort in a large project with several hundred rows of data.

So now if columns are just a way to surface information in the database, how do you remove the data from the database altogether? Select the cells in a column that contain the data you want to delete, and then press **Delete**. Got a lot of rows? Click the first cell in the column, scroll to the last row in the table, press and hold **Shift**, click the last cell in the column, and then press **Delete**. Poof, your data is gone.

 NOTE This might be a good time to point out that Project supports multiple undo levels. That is, you can undo things you did several actions ago by clicking **Undo** or pressing **Ctrl+Z** multiple times. You can set how many undo levels you want to support on a project. On the **File** tab, click **Options**. Click **Advanced**. Under **General**, type the number of undo levels you want to support in the **Undo levels** box, and then click **OK**.

Adding a Column to a View

In any view with data displayed in a table, such as the **Gantt Chart** view, just scroll to the right side of the table portion of the view and you'll see the **Add New Column** header, as shown in Figure 9.2.

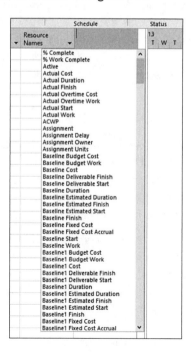

FIGURE 9.2

Click Add New Column to add a column to the current view.

To add a new column, click that header, and then start typing the name of the field you want to add. When you find it in the list, click the name of the column you want to add. After you add the column, you can click and drag to relocate it within the view. Click the new column header to select the column, and then use the four-direction arrow cursor to drag and drop the column within the view.

Alternatively, you can add a column exactly where you want it to appear. Right-click the column header for the column that you want to appear to the right of the column you're adding, and then click **Insert Column**. Click the name of the column to add it to the view.

 NOTE Not sure what field you want to add? A field reference guide is available on Office.com that provides descriptions of each default field included in Project 2013. To use this guide, visit http://office.com/HA102749299.aspx

Hiding a Column in a View

If you want to remove a column from a view without removing the data, click the column header to select the column, and then press **Delete**. Alternatively, you can right-click the column header, and then click **Hide Column**. With either of these options, the data that was entered in that column is not removed from your project. I really cannot emphasize this enough. If you want to remove the data, select the cells containing the data, and then press **Delete**. You'll see the data in the cells is no longer there after you press **Delete**.

Saving a Set of Columns as a Table

The set of columns within a view is called a *table*. For views that contain tables, you can choose from a list of tables to determine what data is displayed. On the **View** tab, in the **Data** group, click **Table** to see the list of available tables for that view. If the existing tables do not meet your needs, you can create a new table that will be available for use in all task views or in all resource views.

You can create a new table in two ways. If you have customized a table in a view by adding or removing columns and want to save that table as a new table, on the **View** tab, in the **Data** group, click **Tables**, and then click **Save Fields as a New Table**. Type a name for the new table, and then click **OK**.

To create a new table from scratch, follow these steps:

1. On the **View** tab, in the **Data** group, click **Tables**, and then click **More Tables**.

2. Click **Task** or **Resource**, depending on what data you're including in the new table (see Figure 9.3).

FIGURE 9.3

Choose to create a task or a resource table.

3. Click **New**, and then type a name for your new table in the **Name** box.

4. Check the **Show in menu** check box, to the right of the **Name** box (as shown in Figure 9.4), if you plan on using the new table often. If you check this check box, the new table will be included in the list that appears when you click **Tables** on the ribbon.

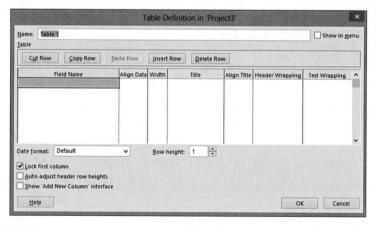

FIGURE 9.4

The Show in menu check box appears to the right of the Name box.

5. Under **Table**, choose which fields you want to include in the table as columns by filling out the **Field Name**, **Align Data**, **Width**, **Title**, **Align Title**, **Header Wrapping**, and **Text Wrapping** columns.

 NOTE You can use the **Cut Row**, **Copy Row**, **Paste Row**, **Insert Row**, and **Delete Row** buttons to edit the list of fields.

6. If you've included any date fields in the new table, click the **Date format** list and choose how you want dates to appear in the table.

7. Type a number in the **Row height** box to adjust row spacing.

8. Check or uncheck the **Lock first column** check box to determine whether you want the first column in the table to be frozen during scrolling.

9. Check or uncheck the **Auto-adjust header row heights** check box to let Project automatically increase or decrease the height of the header row, based on header text length.

10. Check or uncheck the **Show 'Add New Column' interface** check box to determine whether you want to include the ability to add new columns to the table using the far-right column, labeled **Add New Column**.

11. Click **OK** to create the new table.

If you checked the **Show in menu** check box, to display the table, on the **View** tab, in the **Data** group, click **Tables**, and then click the name of the new table.

If you did not select the **Show in menu** check box, to display the table, on the **View** tab, in the **Data** group, click **Tables**, and then click **More Tables**. Click **Task** or **Resource**, depending on which type of table you created. Click the name of the new table, and then click **Apply**.

Creating and Editing Views

If the default views in Project 2013 do not meet your needs, you can make changes to an existing view or create your own. You can create or edit a single view (where one view is displayed in the Project window) or a combination view (where two views are displayed in the Project window at one time).

To create or edit a single view, follow these steps:

1. On the **View** tab, in the **Task Views** or **Resource Views** group, click **Other Views**, and then click **More Views**.

2. If you are editing an existing view, click the name of the view in the list, and then click **Edit**. If you are creating a new view, click **New** (see Figure 9.5).

FIGURE 9.5

Click New or select a view and click Edit.

3. If you are creating a new view, on the **Define New View** dialog box, click **Single view**, and then click **OK**. If you are editing an existing view, skip this step.

4. On the **View Definition** dialog box, edit the following fields:

   - **Name:** Type a name for the view.

   - **Screen:** Choose what type of view you are creating. If you are editing an existing view, you cannot change this option.

   - **Table:** Choose what table you want to display in the view, if the view type you selected includes a table.

   - **Group:** Choose how you want to group data in the view, if the view type you selected includes grouping. If you don't want to group data, click **No Group** in the list.

   - **Filter:** Choose how you want to filter data in the view, if the view type you selected includes filtering. If you don't want to filter data, click **All Tasks** or **All Resources** in the list.

   - **Highlight filter:** Check this check box to highlight the filtered data, instead of hiding data that doesn't meet the filter criteria.

   - **Show in menu:** Check this check box to include the view in the corresponding menu on the **View** tab. For example, if the view type (**Screen**) is **Gantt Chart**, the view will appear in the list when you click **Gantt Chart** on the **View** tab.

NOTE Customizations made to individual views are specific to those views. This includes bar and box styles, in addition to usage view data fields. For example, if you customize the way Gantt bars appear in one view, when you create a new view or go to another view that contains Gantt bars, the customizations will not persist. You'll need to customize the Gantt bars in that view, as well, if you want them to appear the same.

5. Click **OK** to save the view.

A combination view is a view in which two views are displayed in the Project window at one time. For example, the **Task Entry** view, shown in Figure 9.6, is a combination view. It displays the **Gantt Chart** view on the top portion of the screen, and the **Task Form** view on the bottom portion.

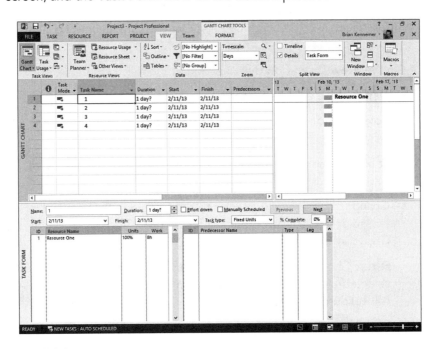

FIGURE 9.6

A combination view with the Gantt Chart on top and the Task Form on the bottom.

To create or edit a combination view, follow these steps:

1. On the **View** tab, in the **Task Views** or **Resource Views** group, click **Other Views**, and then click **More Views**.

2. If you are editing an existing view, click the name of the view in the list, and then click **Edit**. If you are creating a new view, click **New**.

3. If you are creating a new view, in the **Define New View** dialog box, click **Combination view**, and then click **OK**. If you are editing an existing view, skip this step.

4. In the **View Definition** dialog box shown in Figure 9.7, edit the following fields:

   - **Name:** Type a name for the view.

   - **Primary View:** Choose the view you want to display in the top portion of the Project window.

   - **Details Pane:** Choose the view you want to display in the bottom portion of the Project window.

   - **Show in menu:** Check this check box to include the view in the corresponding menu on the **View** tab. For example, if the view type for the primary (top) view is **Gantt Chart**, the view will appear in the list when you click **Gantt Chart** on the **View** tab.

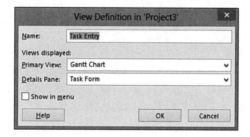

FIGURE 9.7

Define the views to include in your combination view.

5. Click **OK** to save the view.

Another way to save a custom view is to first set up the Project window using the views and tables that you want. With your views set up, on the **View** tab, in the **Task Views** or **Resource Views** group, click **Other Group**, and then click **Save View**. Type a name for the new view, and then click **OK**.

THE ABSOLUTE MINIMUM

Building your own views is an important part of becoming proficient with Project 2013. The built-in views are great, but everyone likes to see things in an order that makes the most sense to them. Take some time and figure out which fields you like to see and in which order and build your own set of views. Custom fields are also a very powerful way to make Project 2013 "your own."

10

UNDERSTANDING PROJECT OPTIONS

The Project Options dialog box provides several choices for controlling how Project 2013 behaves, in addition to how your individual project behaves.

To begin setting the options for your project, click the **File** tab, and then click **Options**, as shown in Figure 10.1.

FIGURE 10.1

Click File, and then click Options.

The sections in this chapter go through each of the option groupings listed on the left side of the Project Options dialog box, as shown in Figure 10.2.

FIGURE 10.2

Options are grouped into tabs on the Project Options dialog box.

General Project Options

The General tab of the Project Options dialog box, as shown in Figure 10.3, includes three sections: User Interface options, Project view, and Personalize your copy of Microsoft Office.

FIGURE 10.3

The General tab of the Project Options dialog box.

User Interface Options

Options listed under User Interface options on the General tab (shown in Figure 10.4) include ScreenTip style, as described in the following section.

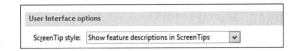

FIGURE 10.4

User Interface options section on the General tab.

ScreenTip Style

ScreenTips are the text that appears when you hover your cursor over various buttons and options within the Project 2013 interface. The ScreenTip style option enables you to choose how you want ScreenTips to behave in Project 2013.

Choose **Show feature descriptions in ScreenTips** to include text that explains the button or option that you are hovering over, as shown in Figure 10.5.

FIGURE 10.5

ScreenTip with feature description.

Choose **Don't show feature descriptions in ScreenTips** to only show the button or option name when hovering over a feature, as shown in Figure 10.6.

FIGURE 10.6

ScreenTip without feature description.

Choose **Don't show ScreenTips** to turn ScreenTips off entirely. With this option selected, hovering over a button or option will not pop up any text.

Project View

Options listed under Project view on the General tab (shown in Figure 10.7) include Default view and Date format, as described in the following sections.

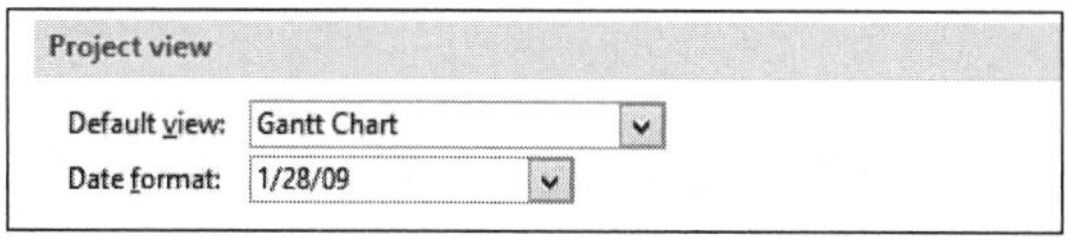

FIGURE 10.7

Project view section on the General tab.

Default View

The default view is the view that displays when you first open a project in Project 2013. If you want the default view to be something other than the **Gantt Chart** view with the timeline displayed, select that view from the **Default view** list. The entire list of Project 2013 views, including any custom views you have created, is included in this list.

Date Format

Choose the format you want to use for dates in your project from the **Date format** list.

Personalize Your Copy of Microsoft Office

Options listed under Personalize your copy of Microsoft Office on the General tab (shown in Figure 10.8) include User name and Initials, as described in the following sections.

FIGURE 10.8

Personalize your copy of Microsoft Office section on the General tab.

User Name

If your name, or the name you want to associate with Project files, differs from the name displayed in this box by default, you can change it here. This name will be populated in the properties for the project. You can, however, change or delete it from the Project Properties dialog box if you would rather not include it with this project file.

Initials

If your initials, or the initials that you want to use to indicate changes you have made to the project, differ from the initials displayed in this box by default, you can change them here.

Always Use These Values Regardless of Sign In to Office

You can now sign in to Office 2013 with a Microsoft Live account. This can help you more easily connect Office with your Office 365 account. This option allows you to specify whether Project should use the name and initials specified in this section or if it should use your name information from your Live account.

Office Background and Office Theme

Office 2013 by default has a very lightly colored theme. It gives the apps a very clean look, but for some people this color scheme can make it difficult to navigate. You can pick Dark Gray or Light Gray from the Office Theme option to give the ribbon and other parts of the application a bit of a background color.

Office Background allows you to pick from a variety of decorative patterns that will be drawn against this background.

Startup Options

Show the Start Screen When This Application Starts

With this option checked, Project 2013 opens to a screen that shows you recently opened files and lists commonly used templates. If you uncheck this option, Project opens directly to a blank project in your default view.

Display Options

The Display tab of the Project Options dialog box, as shown in Figure 10.9, includes four sections: Calendar, Currency options for this project, Show indicators and options buttons for, and Show these elements.

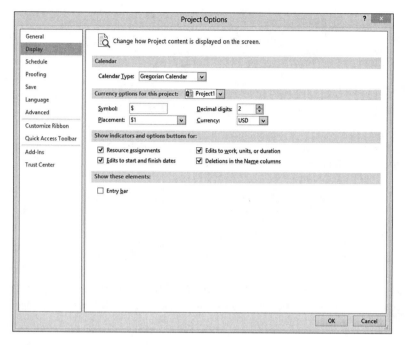

FIGURE 10.9

The Display tab of the Project Options dialog box.

Calendar

Under **Calendar**, choose the **Calendar Type** you want to use for your project. You can choose from **Gregorian Calendar**, **Hijri Calendar**, or **Thai Buddhist Calendar**. Figure 10.10 shows the Calendar section.

FIGURE 10.10

Calendar section on the Display tab.

Currency Options for This Project

You can choose to apply the options listed under **Currency** options for this project, on the **Display** tab (shown in Figure 10.11), to a specific project, as opposed to broadly, for all projects you work with in Project 2013.

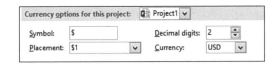

FIGURE 10.11

Currency options for this project section on the Display tab.

To choose which project to apply these options to, click the name of the project in the list included in the section header, as shown in Figure 10.12.

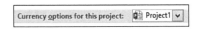

FIGURE 10.12

Choose which project these options apply to.

Options listed under Currency options for this project include Symbol, Decimal digits, Placement, and Currency, as described in the following sections.

Symbol

Type the symbol to use for currency values. For example, if your project primarily deals in dollars, type the **$** symbol in this box.

Decimal Digits

Type the number of digits to include after the decimal point in currency values. For example, if you set this value to **2**, a currency value might look like this: $12,345.67.

Placement

Choose where you want the symbol to appear, in relation to the currency number. You can choose to include it to the immediate left or right of the number ($1 or 1$), or include a space between the symbol and the number ($ 1 or 1 $).

Currency

Choose the currency that the project primarily uses. If you have individual values to add to your project that use a currency other than the default you set here, you will need to convert that value before adding it to your project.

Show Indicators and Options Buttons For

Check or uncheck the check boxes under **Show indicators and options buttons for** (shown in Figure 10.13) to control when you want a contextual menu to appear when you've made changes to fields in your project. These check boxes include **Resource assignments**; **Edits to work, units, or duration**; **Edits to start and finish dates**; and **Deletions in the Name columns**.

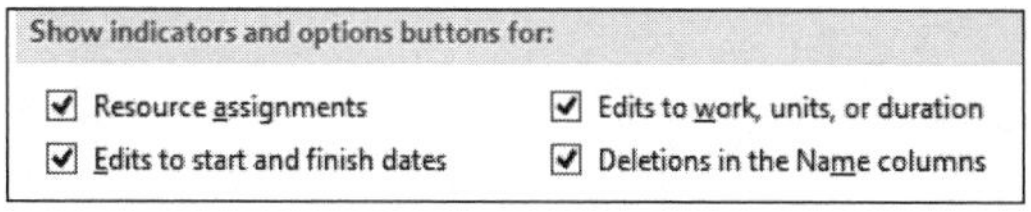

FIGURE 10.13

Show indicators and options buttons for section on the Display tab.

The best practice here is to check all of these check boxes because these messages can be very helpful for any level of Project user.

Show These Elements

Under **Show these elements** (shown in Figure 10.14), check the **Entry bar** check box to add a text entry field above the view where you're entering data, similar to entering data in an Excel spreadsheet.

FIGURE 10.14

Show these elements section on the Display tab.

Figure 10.15 shows the entry bar in the **Gantt Chart** view.

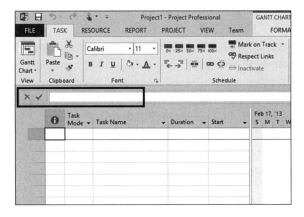

FIGURE 10.15

The entry bar is displayed above the grid in a view.

Schedule Options

The Schedule tab of the Project Options dialog box, as shown in Figure 10.16, includes six sections: Calendar options for this project, Schedule, Scheduling options for this project, Schedule Alerts Options, Calculation, and Calculation options for this project.

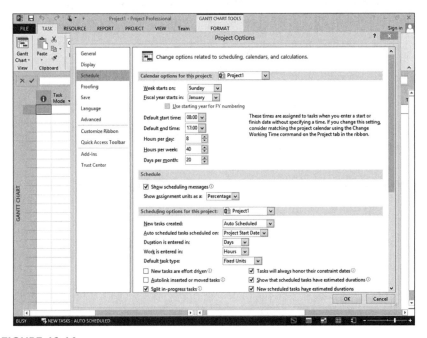

FIGURE 10.16

The Schedule tab of the Project Options dialog box.

Calendar Options for This Project

You can choose to apply the options listed under Calendar options for this project, on the Schedule tab (shown in Figure 10.17), to a specific project. To choose which project to apply these options to, click the name of the project in the list included in the section header.

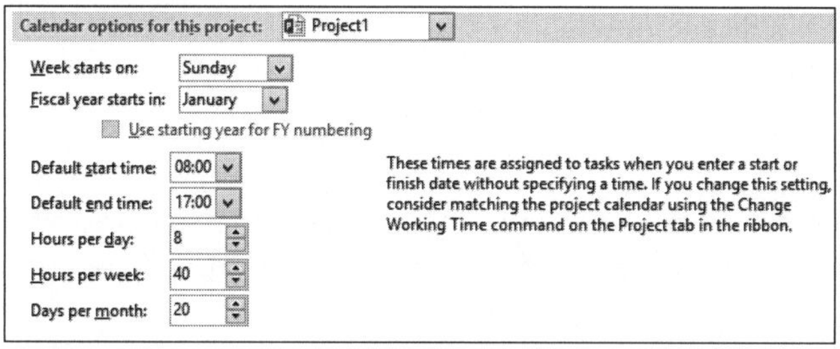

FIGURE 10.17

Calendar options for this project section on the Schedule tab.

Options listed under Calendar options for this project are described in the following sections.

Week Starts On

Choose the day that begins each week in the selected project. For example, some organizations may consider Monday the first day of the week, whereas other organizations may consider Sunday to be the first day of the week. Setting this option controls how calendars are displayed in the selected project.

Take care when changing this setting. It is generally best to pick an organizational standard and stick with that setting. Moving between projects where this setting is different can be confusing when working with calendar displays.

Fiscal Year Starts In

Choose the first month of the fiscal year for the selected project. The fiscal year is the 12-month period used for accounting purposes, and may be the same as, or different from, the calendar year.

Use Starting Year for FY Numbering

If you choose any month other than January from the **Fiscal year starts in** list, the **Use starting year for FY numbering** check box becomes available. This is because a fiscal year that begins midway through a calendar year will include some months during the first calendar year and other months during the second calendar year. For example, if my fiscal year starts in November 2014, November and December will be in calendar year 2014, and the rest of my fiscal year (January through October) will be in calendar year 2015.

If you want to use the first calendar year as the year included in fiscal year numbering, check the **Use starting year for FY numbering** check box. For example, if I check this check box, the numbering for a fiscal year that starts in November 2014 will continue to be FY14, even though the months actually fall in the 2015 calendar year.

Default Start Time

Choose the start time for a typical work day in the selected project. If necessary, you can adjust this start time for specific tasks or resources within the project.

Default End Time

Choose the finish time for a typical work day in the selected project. If necessary, you can adjust this finish time for specific tasks or resources within the project.

Hours per Day

Type the number of hours that resources in the selected project typically put in during a work day. If necessary, you can adjust the number of work hours for specific tasks or resources within the project. This value is used to convert duration and work values. For example, if you enter a duration value of 12 hours and this setting is set to 8, Project interprets your entry as 1.5 days. Likewise, an entry of 1.5 days would be seen as 12 hours.

Hours per Week

Type the number of hours that resources in the selected project typically put in during a work week. Similar to Hours per day, this is used to convert hours to weeks and weeks to hours. If this setting is set to 40 hours and you enter a duration of 1.5 weeks, Project sees that as equal to 60 hours.

Days per Month

Type the number of working days in a month for the selected project. This is another example of a conversion factor. It is used to convert days to months and months to days. If this setting is 20 days and you enter 2 months, Project sees this as 40 days.

NOTE   It is generally a good idea to make sure that these settings match up with the settings in your Project base calendar. If your calendar work week settings start at 9 a.m. but these settings start at 8 a.m., the Gantt Chart may seem to draw the start times of Gantt bars incorrectly. Similarly, if the hours per day, hours per week, and days per month settings here differ from the data set in your calendar, work and duration values for tasks may appear incorrect and could cause confusion.

Schedule

Options listed under Schedule on the Schedule tab (shown in Figure 10.18) include Show scheduling messages and Show assignment units as a, as described in the following sections.

FIGURE 10.18

Schedule section on the Schedule tab.

Show Scheduling Messages

Check this check box to display messages indicating inconsistencies in your plan while you work with your project. For example, if you change your project so that a successor task starts before a predecessor task has finished, a message will be displayed to alert you of that inconsistency.

If you are a newcomer to Project, it is a good idea to keep this box checked.

Show Assignment Units as A

Choose whether you want to show assignment units as a percentage or a decimal. Assignment units represent how much of a resource's time is currently assigned to a specific task or project.

Scheduling Options for This Project

You can choose to apply the options listed under Scheduling options for this project, on the Schedule tab (shown in Figure 10.19), to a specific project. To choose which project to apply these options to, click the name of the project in the list included in the section header.

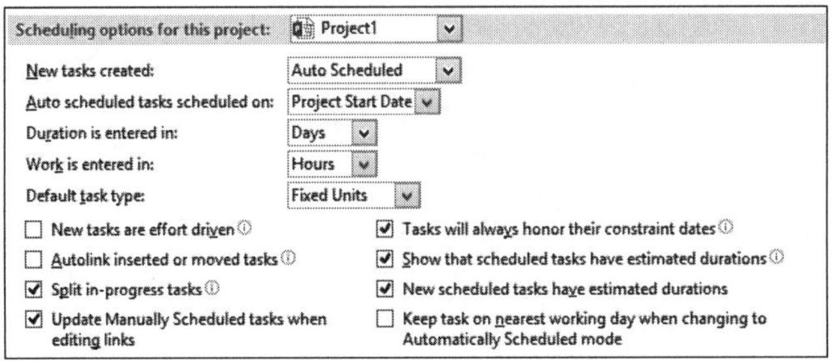

FIGURE 10.19

Scheduling options for this project section on the Schedule tab.

Options listed under Scheduling options for this project are described in the following sections.

New Tasks Created

Choose whether you want new tasks in your project to be **Auto Scheduled**, using the Project scheduling engine, or **Manually Scheduled**, using only the dates you enter. You can change this setting for each task individually. What you choose here simply sets what the default is for each new task in your project.

Auto Scheduled Tasks Scheduled On

Choose whether you want to use the **Project Start Date** or the **Current Date** as the default start date for new tasks in your project.

Duration Is Entered In

Choose the time units you want to use, by default, when identifying the length of time you think tasks in your project will take (also known as *duration*). You can choose **Minutes, Hours, Days, Weeks,** or **Months**. You can choose any of these time units at any time when entering task durations. Here, you're simply setting what the default is for each new task in your project. Generally, duration is expressed in days.

Work Is Entered In

Choose the time units you want to use, by default, when entering the work completed on tasks in your project. As with duration, you can choose **Minutes, Hours, Days, Weeks,** or **Months**, and you are choosing the default unit for new tasks. Generally, work is expressed in hours, though sometimes days are more appropriate.

Default Task Type

Choose what task type you want to use, by default, for new tasks in your project. You can manually change this on a per-task basis.

New Tasks Are Effort Driven

Check this check box to maintain work values for tasks in your project, by default, as you add or remove assignments. You can manually change this on a per-task basis.

Autolink Inserted or Moved Tasks

Check this check box to automatically link tasks when you insert, delete, or move tasks between existing Finish-to-Start links. For example, suppose that you have two tasks that are linked, and you right-click the second task to insert another task between them. The inserted task maintains the link structure so that it is linked to the task above it as well as the task below it.

Split In-Progress Tasks

Check this check box to allow Project to reschedule remaining duration and work on tasks, as necessary.

Update Manually Scheduled Tasks when Editing Links

Check this check box to include updates to manually scheduled tasks when making changes to links between tasks.

Tasks Will Always Honor Their Constraint Dates

Check this check box to require that Project always maintain constraint dates for tasks in your project.

For example, if a task has a constraint set so that it must start on 11/4/13, and if the Tasks will always honor their constraint dates check box is checked, you can choose to ignore the links, lag, and lead time between that task and other tasks and maintain the constraint. The task will start on 11/4/13, no matter what.

If the Tasks will always honor their constraint dates check box is cleared, the relationship that a task has with other tasks will determine the schedule, even if a constraint is set. So, if a task has a constraint set so that it must start on 11/4/13, but it's also linked so that it starts after another task, and that other task doesn't finish until 11/12/13, the constraint date will be ignored.

Show That Scheduled Tasks Have Estimated Durations

Check this check box to display a question mark (?) after duration values that are estimated, as opposed to manually entered in the project.

New Scheduled Tasks Have Estimated Durations

Check this check box to initially use estimated durations for tasks in your project. Estimated durations are those that Project has determined based on other scheduling factors in your plan.

Keep Task on Nearest Working Day When Changing to Automatically Scheduled Mode

Check this check box to align tasks with working days in your calendar when switching those tasks from being manually scheduled to being automatically scheduled. Manually scheduled tasks may be scheduled over nonworking days. When you switch those tasks to automatic scheduling, if this check box is checked, the tasks are moved to the nearest possible working day.

Schedule Alerts Options

You can choose to apply the options listed under Schedule Alerts Options, on the Schedule tab (shown in Figure 10.20), to a specific project. To choose which project to apply these options to, click the name of the project in the list included in the section header.

FIGURE 10.20

Schedule Alerts Options section on the Schedule tab.

Under **Schedule Alerts Options**, select the **Show task schedule warnings** and/or **Show task schedule suggestions** check boxes to display a warning message and/or suggested options when Project identifies a possible scheduling conflict with a manually scheduled task.

I highly recommend having both of these options checked if you are new to using Project. The warnings and suggestions can be quite helpful.

Calculation

Under Calculation, on the Schedule tab (shown in Figure 10.21), choose whether you want Project to recalculate your schedule after every edit.

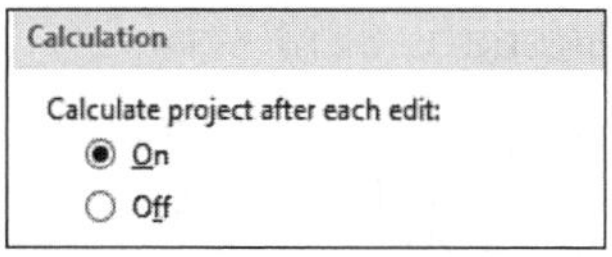

FIGURE 10.21

Calculation section on the Schedule tab.

If you choose Off, you must manually recalculate your schedule. On the **Project** tab, in the **Schedule** group, click **Calculate Project**. Choosing to turn calculation off is rare and should be performed only by advanced Project users.

Calculation Options for This Project

You can choose to apply the options listed under Calculation options for this project, on the Schedule tab (shown in Figure 10.22), to a specific project. To choose which project to apply these options to, click the name of the project in the list included in the section header.

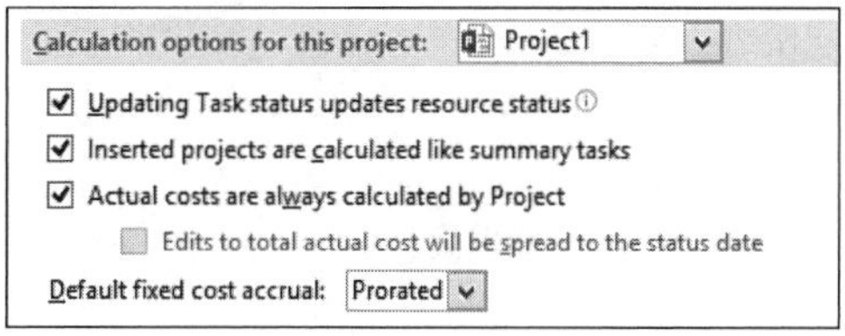

FIGURE 10.22

Calculation options for this project section on the Schedule tab.

Options listed under Calculation options for this project are described in the following sections.

Updating Task Status Updates Resource Status

Check this check box to automatically update resource assignment status data, such as remaining work, whenever you update task status data, such as percent complete. With this check box checked, updates to assignment status data will also automatically update task status data. Generally only advanced users should uncheck this box.

Inserted Projects Are Calculated Like Summary Tasks

Check this check box to use the same rollup rules for inserted projects as are used for summary tasks.

Actual Costs Are Always Calculated by Project

Check this check box to require that actual cost calculation be done only by Project, not manually. If you check this check box, additional actual costs can only be added manually after the task is 100% complete. The best practice here is to leave this check box checked. Clearing it is for advanced users only.

Edits to Total Actual Cost Will Be Spread to the Status Date

Check this check box to evenly distribute actual costs across the project's schedule, to the status date. This check box is only available if the Actual costs are always calculated by Project check box is cleared.

Default Fixed Cost Accrual

Choose whether you want fixed costs to be incurred at the start of a task, at the end of a task, or prorated across the entire duration of a task.

Proofing Options

The Proofing tab of the Project Options dialog box, as shown in Figure 10.23, includes three sections: AutoCorrect options, When correcting spelling in Microsoft Office programs, and When correcting spelling in Project.

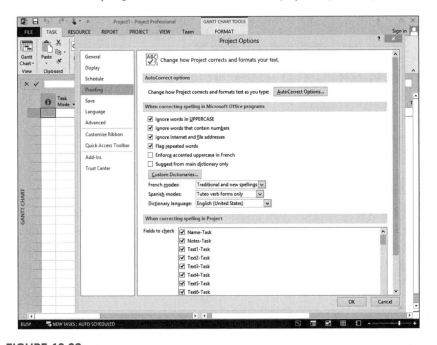

FIGURE 10.23

The Proofing tab of the Project Options dialog box.

AutoCorrect Options

Click **AutoCorrect Options**, in the **AutoCorrect Options** section of the **Proofing** tab (shown in Figure 10.24), to change how Project 2013 corrects and formats the text you enter as you plan your project.

FIGURE 10.24

AutoCorrect Options section on the Proofing tab.

When Correcting Spelling in Microsoft Office Programs

Set the options in the **When correcting spelling in Microsoft Office programs** section on the **Proofing** tab (shown in Figure 10.25) to determine how all Microsoft Office applications (including Project) handle unique spelling issues.

FIGURE 10.25

When correcting spelling in Microsoft Office Programs section on the Proofing tab.

When Correcting Spelling in Project

Choose which Project fields to include in spell check by checking or unchecking the check boxes listed under **When correcting spelling in Project**, on the **Proofing** tab (shown in Figure 10.26).

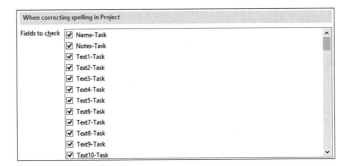

FIGURE 10.26

When correcting spelling in Project section on the Proofing tab.

Save Options

The Save tab of the Project Options dialog box, as shown in Figure 10.27, includes three sections: Save projects, Save templates, and Cache.

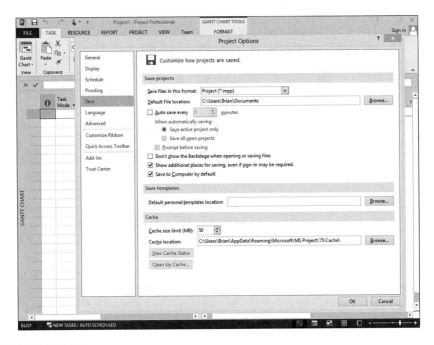

FIGURE 10.27

The Save tab of the Project Options dialog box.

Save Projects

Options listed under Save projects, on the Save tab (shown in Figure 10.28), include Save files in this format, Default File location, and Auto save every, as described in the following sections.

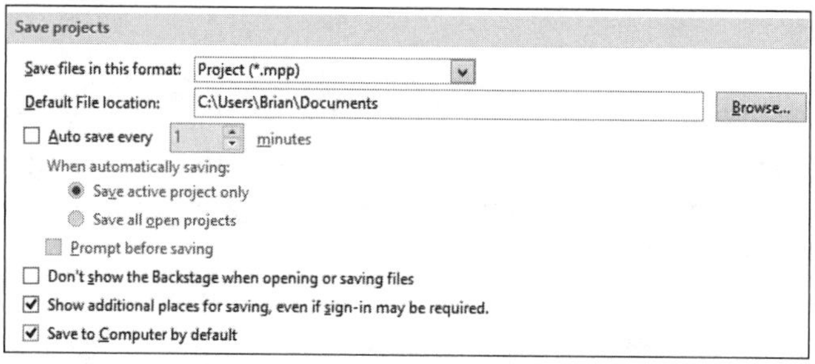

FIGURE 10.28

Save projects section on the Save tab.

Save Files in This Format

Choose the default file format for saving project files. You can choose from **Project (*.mpp), Microsoft Project 2007 (*.mpp), Microsoft Project 2000 – 2003 (*.mpp),** and **Project Template (*.mpt).** You can choose to save in any of these formats at any point. Here, you are simply choosing which format to use, by default.

Default File Location

Enter the path to the default location where you typically save your project files. You can type the path directly in the box, or you can click **Browse** to navigate to the location. You can choose to save to any appropriate location at any point. Here, you are simply choosing where to save files, by default.

Auto Save Every

Check this check box if you want Project 2013 to automatically save your project periodically. You can set the save interval in minutes and then choose whether you want to save just the project you're currently working in or all open projects, and you can choose whether you want to be prompted before Project saves the corresponding files.

Don't Show the Backstage When Opening or Saving Files

By default, this option is unchecked. This means that if you click Save or Open, Project displays the backstage screen that gives you some advanced options for saving to or opening from SharePoint or Office365 installations. If you prefer to have Project display the standard Windows Open and Save dialogs, check this option.

Show Additional Places for Saving, Even If Sign-In May Be Required

This is another option that has to do with saving to or opening from SharePoint or Office365 installations. Check this option if you want to see the more advanced save and open locations.

Save to Computer by Default

With this option unchecked, Project defaults the save location to be your connected SharePoint or Office365 installation.

Save Templates

Under **Save templates**, on the **Save** tab (shown in Figure 10.29), enter the path where you want to save Project templates (.mpt files) by default. You can type the path to the location, or click **Browse** to navigate to the location. You can choose to save a Project template to another location at any point. Here, you are simply choosing the default location for template files.

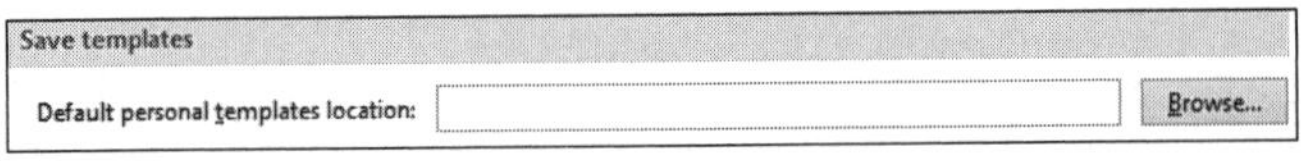

FIGURE 10.29

Save templates section on the Save tab.

Cache

Under **Cache**, on the **Save** tab (shown in Figure 10.30), set the size and location for the cache used by Project Professional 2013 when connected to Project Server. This is the portion of your hard drive that is used to save server files locally, making for faster project editing and saving when connected to Project Server.

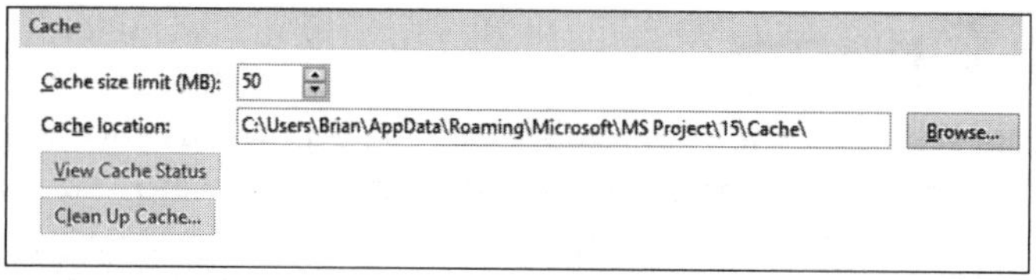

FIGURE 10.30

Cache section on the Save tab.

Language Options

The Language tab of the Project Options dialog box, as shown in Figure 10.31, is used to set the editing languages, and display and Help languages, for all Microsoft Office applications, including Project.

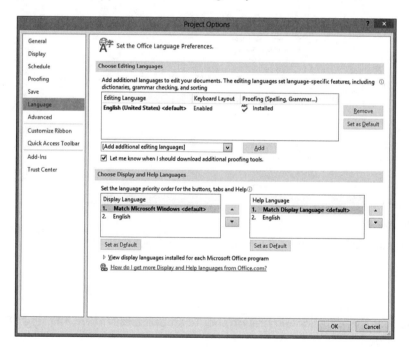

FIGURE 10.31

The Language tab of the Project Options dialog box.

Advanced Options

The Advanced tab of the Project Options dialog box, as shown in Figure 10.32, includes 10 sections: General, Project Web App, Planning Wizard, General options for this project, Edit, Display, Display options for this project, Cross project linking options for this project, Earned Value options for this project, and Calculation options for this project.

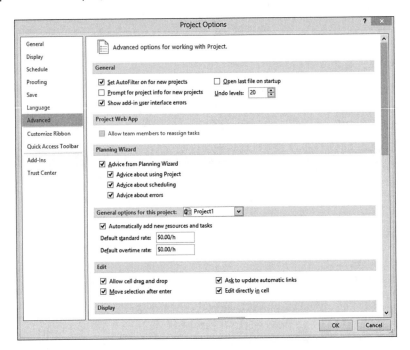

FIGURE 10.32

The Advanced tab of the Project Options dialog box.

General

Options listed under General on the Advanced tab (shown in Figure 10.33) are described in the following sections.

General	
☑ Set AutoFilter on for new projects	☐ Open last file on startup
☐ Prompt for project info for new projects	Undo levels: 20
☑ Show add-in user interface errors	

FIGURE 10.33

General section on the Advanced tab.

Set AutoFilter On for New Projects

Check this check box to turn on the ability to filter using column headers, by default. Figure 10.34 shows a column header with AutoFilter turned on.

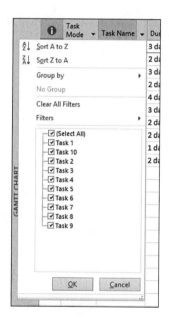

FIGURE 10.34

AutoFilter enables you to look for specific data in a column.

Prompt for Project Info for New Projects

Check this check box to immediately open the Project Information dialog box when creating a new project. Figure 10.35 shows the Project Information dialog box.

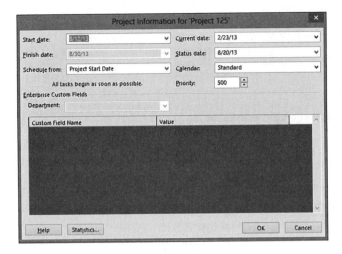

FIGURE 10.35

The Project Information dialog box.

Show Add-In User Interface Errors

Check this check box to display error messages when an add-in fails to work properly, in a way that relates to the Project 2013 user interface.

Open Last File on Startup

With this check box checked, when you open Project 2013, the same file that was open when you closed Project will reopen. This can be helpful if you work primarily in one project file at a time.

Undo Levels

Type the number of times you want to be able to click Undo. Consider performance when choosing this number. Under some circumstances having a high number set here can slow down system performance. This is generally when there is a very large number of tasks and the edits you are making impact large numbers of tasks. Having to store multiple levels going back 70 or 80 times can start to take up system memory.

Project Web App

If your organization uses Project Professional 2013 with Project Server, select the **Allow team members to reassign tasks** check box, under **Project Web App** on the **Advanced** tab (shown in Figure 10.36), to determine whether resources on a project can reassign their tasks to other resources, using Project Web App.

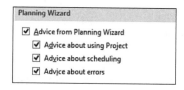

FIGURE 10.36

Project Web App section on the Advanced tab.

Planning Wizard

Check the check boxes under **Planning Wizard** on the **Advanced** tab (shown in Figure 10.37) to choose what tips you want to display to help you plan your project. You can choose to display tips about using Project, scheduling, and errors. If you don't want to display any tips, uncheck the **Advice from Planning Wizard** check box.

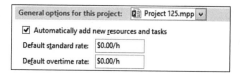

FIGURE 10.37

Planning Wizard section on the Advanced tab.

General Options for This Project

You can choose to apply the options listed under **General options for this project**, on the **Advanced** tab (shown in Figure 10.38), to a specific project. To choose which project to apply these options to, click the name of the project in the list included in the section header.

FIGURE 10.38

General options for this project section on the Advanced tab.

Options listed under General options for this project are described in the following sections.

Automatically Add New Resources and Tasks

Check this check box to automatically add resources and tasks to the project and resource sheet as you assign work. If this check box is unchecked, you will be alerted each time a new resource or task is added to your project through an assignment.

Default Standard Rate

Type a value to use as a standard pay rate for all new resources, by default. This proves helpful if many resources use a common pay rate. You can adjust pay rates for individual resources.

Default Overtime Rate

Type a value to use as a default overtime pay rate for new resources. You can adjust overtime rates for individual resources.

Edit

Options listed under Edit on the Advanced tab (shown in Figure 10.39) are described in the following sections.

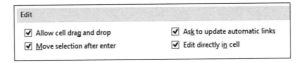

FIGURE 10.39

Edit section on the Advanced tab.

Allow Cell Drag and Drop

Check this check box to be able to drag data from one cell or row and drop it in another.

Move Selection After Enter

With this check box checked, pressing **Enter** after typing in a cell moves the cursor to the next row.

Ask to Update Automatic Links

With this check box checked, when you open a project that contains a link to another project, and that other project has been modified, a prompt will ask if you want to update your project with those changes.

Edit Directly in Cell

Check this check box to be able to type directly in cells. If this check box is cleared, be sure to check the **Entry bar** check box on the **Display** tab.

Display

Options listed under Display on the Advanced tab (shown in Figure 10.40) are described in the following sections.

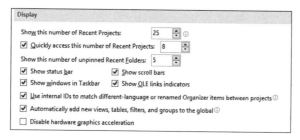

FIGURE 10.40

Display section on the Advanced tab.

Show This Number of Recent Projects

Under **Display**, type the number of documents you want listed when you click the **File** tab, and then click **Recent**. Figure 10.41 shows the list of recent documents.

FIGURE 10.41

Recent documents on the File tab.

Show Status Bar

Check this check box to display messages about what Project 2013 is doing, or what actions you might need to take, at the bottom of the Project window. Figure 10.42 shows the status bar.

FIGURE 10.42

Status bar.

Show Windows in Taskbar

Check this check box to show each Project window as a separate button on the Windows taskbar.

Use Internal IDs to Match Different-Language or Renamed Organizer Items Between Projects

Check this check box to match Organizer elements using internal IDs, instead of words. This proves helpful if you are working in multiple languages. The Organizer dialog box, shown in Figure 10.43, is used to synchronize different Project elements between multiple files or between Project Server and local Project files.

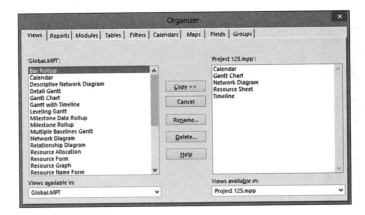

FIGURE 10.43

The Organizer dialog box.

To access the Organizer dialog box, click the **File** tab, click **Info**, and then click **Organizer**.

Automatically Add New Views, Tables, Filters, and Groups to the Global

Check this check box to automatically add these items to the global project template, making them available in all projects, instead of just the current project.

Show Scrollbars

Check this check box to display scrollbars at the far right and bottom of the Project window.

Show OLE Links Indicators

Check this check box to display an indicator for items that are OLE linked within your project. This means that the data in your project is copied from, and linked to, data in another project. Figure 10.44 shows an OLE link indicator.

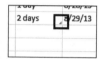

FIGURE 10.44

The gray triangle in the bottom right is an OLE indicator.

Display Options for This Project

You can choose to apply the options listed under Display options for this project, on the Advanced tab (shown in Figure 10.45), to a specific project. To choose which project to apply these options to, click the name of the project in the list included in the section header.

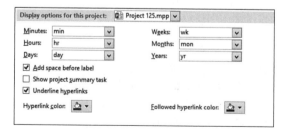

FIGURE 10.45

Display options for this project section on the Advanced tab.

Options listed under Display options for this project are described in the following sections.

Minutes, Hours, Days, Weeks, Months, and Years

Set the abbreviations you want to use for **Minutes**, **Hours**, **Days**, **Weeks**, **Months**, and **Years**.

Add Space Before Label

Check this check box to insert a space between the number value and the time abbreviation (for example, 1 wk, as opposed to 1wk).

Show Project Summary Task

Check this check box to display a row at the top of your project that summarizes all project data in each column currently displayed. Figure 10.46 shows a project with the project summary task displayed.

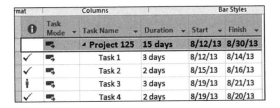

FIGURE 10.46

The top row displays the project summary task.

Underline Hyperlinks

Check this check box to use underlining to visually indicate hyperlinks. Select **Hyperlink color** and **Followed hyperlink color** if you want to use something other than the default blue and purple.

Cross Project Linking Options for This Project

You can choose to apply the options listed under Cross project linking options for this project, on the Advanced tab (shown in Figure 10.47), to a specific project. To choose which project to apply these options to, click the name of the project in the list included in the section header.

Cross project linking options for this project:	📊 Project 125.mpp ▾
☑ Show external successors	☑ Show 'Links Between Projects' dialog box on open
☑ Show external predecessors	☐ Automatically accept new external data

FIGURE 10.47

Cross project linking options for this project section on the Advanced tab.

Options listed under Cross project linking options for this project are described in the following sections.

Show External Successors

Check this check box to show tasks from other linked projects that are successors to tasks in your project.

Show External Predecessors

Check this check box to show tasks from other linked projects that are predecessors to tasks in your project.

Show 'Links Between Projects' Dialog Box on Open

Check this check box to immediately display the Links Between Projects dialog box when you open a project that contains links to other projects.

Automatically Accept New External Data

Check this check box to automatically add changes to dependencies between tasks in separate projects. This check box is only available when the Show Links Between Projects dialog box on open check box is cleared.

Earned Value Options for This Project

You can choose to apply the options listed under Earned Value options for this project, on the Advanced tab (shown in Figure 10.48), to a specific project. To choose which project to apply these options to, click the name of the project in the list included in the section header.

FIGURE 10.48

Earned Value options for this project section on the Advanced tab.

Options listed under Earned Value options for this project are described in the following sections.

Default Task Earned Value Method

Choose whether you want to use **% Complete** or **Physical % Complete** for earned value calculations.

Baseline for Earned Value Calculation

Choose which baseline you want to use for analyzing earned value in your project.

Calculation Options for This Project

You can choose to apply the options listed under Calculation options for this project, on the Advanced tab (shown in Figure 10.49), to a specific project. To choose which project to apply these options to, click the name of the project in the list included in the section header.

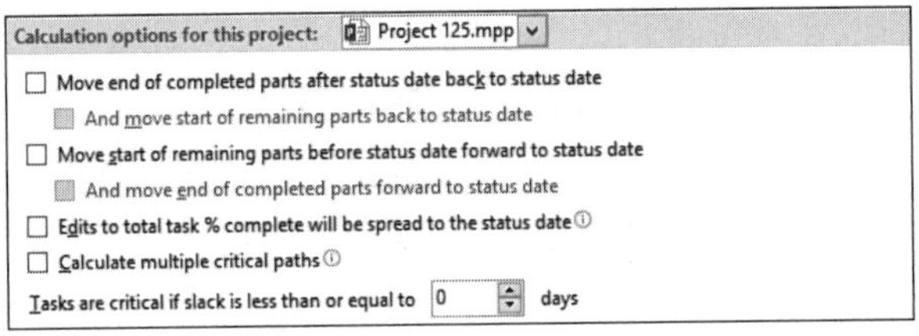

FIGURE 10.49

Calculation options for this project section on the Advanced tab.

Options listed under Calculation options for this project are described in the following sections.

Move End of Completed Parts After Status Date Back to Status Date

Check this check box to move actual completed work that was finished prior to the status date, so that the completed portion finishes on the status date. The remainder will continue to be scheduled as planned.

And Move Start of Remaining Parts Back to Status Date

Check this check box to move the remainder of a task that started early up to start at the status date. This check box is only available if the Move end of completed parts after status date back to status check box is checked.

Move Start of Remaining Parts Before Status Date Forward to Status Date

Check this check box to move remaining work on a task that started late, so that it starts on the status date.

And Move End of Completed Parts Forward to Status Date

Check this check box to move completed work on a task that started late, so that the completed portion finishes on the status date. This check box is available only if the Move start of remaining parts before status date forward to status date check box is checked.

Edits to Total Task % Complete Will Be Spread to the Status Date

Check this check box to evenly distribute changes to total % complete across the schedule to the status date.

Calculate Multiple Critical Paths

Check this check box to calculate the critical path for each set of linked tasks in your project.

Tasks Are Critical If Slack Is Less Than or Equal To

Type a number of days of slack. Tasks with this many, or fewer, days of slack will be identified as critical.

Customize Ribbon Options

The Customize Ribbon tab of the Project Options dialog box, as shown in Figure 10.50, enables you to change the buttons and other options that appear on each of the tabs of the ribbon in Project 2013. You can also create new tabs, new groups, and other options.

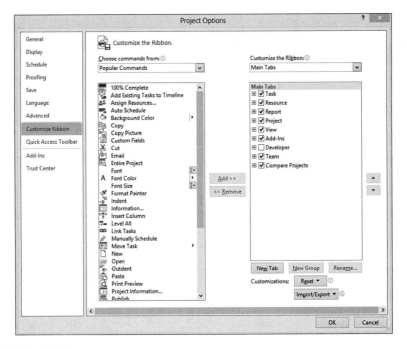

FIGURE 10.50

The Customize Ribbon tab of the Project Options dialog box.

Customize the Ribbon

You can customize the ribbon several different ways. The following procedures walk you through adding a command to an existing ribbon tab, creating a new tab, and creating a new group on a tab.

To add a command to an existing tab, follow these steps:

1. Click the **File** tab, and then click **Options**.

2. On the **Project Options** dialog box, click the **Customize Ribbon** tab.

3. On the **Customize Ribbon** tab, choose **All Tabs** from the **Customize the Ribbon** list, and then expand the name of the tab in the box on the right. Groups on the tab are listed below the tab name.

4. Click the group where you want to add the new command to select it.

5. Under **Choose commands from**, click **All Commands**.

NOTE If you know what type of command you want to add to the selected group, choose a command type from the **Choose commands from** list. This will narrow the list of commands, making it easier for you to find what you're looking for.

6. Click the name of the command you want to add to the selected group, and then click **Add** to move it to that group.

7. To reorder the commands within a group, select the command you want to move, and then use the up and down arrow buttons to the right of the Customize the Ribbon box to move the selected command up or down in the list.

To create and rename a new tab, follow these steps:

1. Click the **File** tab, and then click **Options**.

2. On the **Project Options** dialog box, click the **Customize Ribbon** tab.

3. On the **Customize Ribbon** tab, choose **All Tabs** from the **Customize the Ribbon** list.

4. Click the name of the existing tab that you want to appear just before the new tab. For example, if you want to create a new tab between the **Task** and **Resource** tabs, click the **Task** tab. The new tab will be created after the **Task** tab.

5. Click **New Tab**. A new tab and new group are created.

6. Click **New Tab (Custom)**, and then click **Rename**.

7. Type a name for the new tab in the **Display name** box, and then click **OK**.

8. Repeat steps 6 and 7 to rename the new group on the new tab.

To create and rename a new group, follow these steps:

1. Click the **File** tab, and then click **Options**.

2. On the **Project Options** dialog box, click the **Customize Ribbon** tab.

3. On the **Customize Ribbon** tab, choose **All Tabs** from the **Customize the Ribbon** list, and then expand the name of the tab where you want to create the new group in the box on the right. Groups on the tab are listed below the tab name.

4. Click the name of the existing group that you want to appear just before the new group. For example, if you want to create a new group between the **Insert** and **Properties** groups, click the **Insert** group. The new group will be created after the **Insert** tab.

5. Click **New Group**.

6. Click **New Group (Custom)**, and then click **Rename**.

7. Type a name for the new group in the **Display name** box, and then click **OK**.

Quick Access Toolbar Options

The Quick Access Toolbar tab of the Project Options dialog box, as shown in Figure 10.51, enables you to choose which options you want to include on the Quick Access toolbar.

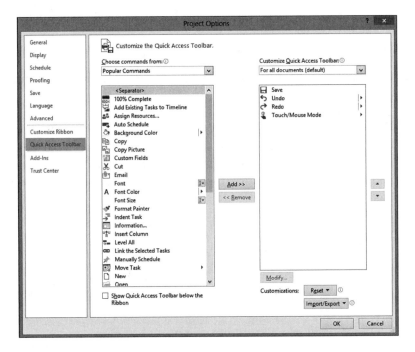

FIGURE 10.51

The Quick Access Toolbar tab of the Project Options dialog box.

The Quick Access toolbar appears at the very top of the Project window, next to the Save, Undo, and Redo buttons. Figure 10.52 shows the Quick Access toolbar.

FIGURE 10.52

The Quick Access toolbar appears at the top of the Project window.

If you select the **Show Quick Access Toolbar below the Ribbon** check box on the **Quick Access Toolbar** tab, the Quick Access toolbar appears, as shown in Figure 10.53.

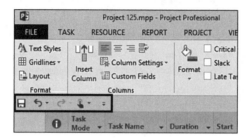

FIGURE 10.53

You can also display the Quick Access toolbar below the ribbon.

Customize the Quick Access Toolbar

To add a command to the Quick Access toolbar, follow these steps:

1. Click the **File** tab, and then click **Options**.

2. On the **Project Options** dialog box, click the **Quick Access Toolbar** tab.

3. On the **Quick Access Toolbar** tab, choose **All Commands** from the **Choose commands from** list.

 NOTE If you know what type of command you want to add to the Quick Access toolbar, choose a command type from the **Choose commands from** list. This will narrow the list of commands, making it easier for you to find what you're looking for.

4. Click the name of the command you want to add to the Quick Access toolbar, and then click **Add** to move it to the box on the right.

5. To reorder the commands on the Quick Access toolbar, select the command you want to move from the box on the right, and then use the up and down arrow buttons to the right of the box to move the selected command up or

down in the list. This moves the command left or right on the Quick Access toolbar.

Add-Ins Options

The Add-Ins tab of the Project Options dialog box, as shown in Figure 10.54, enables you to manage and view the add-ins used throughout all Microsoft Office applications.

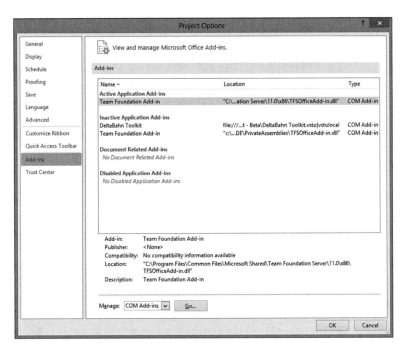

FIGURE 10.54

The Add-Ins tab of the Project Options dialog box.

To make changes to your add-ins, at the bottom of the **Add-Ins** tab, choose the add-in type from the **Manage** list, and then click **Go**. You can also see a list of disabled add-ins. Click **Disabled Items** from the **Manage** list, and then click **Go**.

Trust Center Options

The Trust Center tab of the Project Options dialog box, as shown in Figure 10.55, provides information about privacy, security, and the Microsoft Project Trust Center.

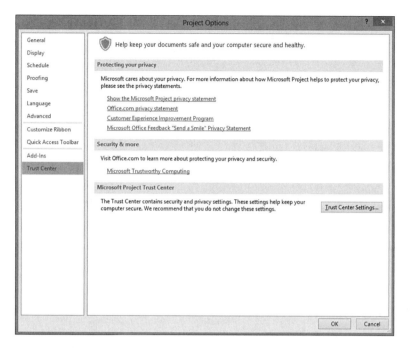

FIGURE 10.55

The Trust Center tab of the Project Options dialog box.

Although you are able to modify Trust Center settings on this tab, the best practice is to leave them alone and use the default settings.

THE ABSOLUTE MINIMUM

As you can see, there are many, many options in Project 2013. Some of them, like the ones that concern formatting, are not really key to your use of Project and how you schedule, whereas others, such as the Hours-Per-Day setting, can have a direct impact on how things like duration or work are calculated. A key takeaway from this chapter is to remember that when you are thinking about changing a setting, do it in a test project first. Test the impact on your schedule, and if everything is okay, make the change in your real schedule.

11

DEALING WITH PROBLEMS

This chapter covers how you can use Project 2013 to resolve common problems with your project.

While managing projects, you will undoubtedly run into any number of problems. This book has provided you with many of the processes for dealing with basic problems, such as splitting tasks and reassigning work to other resources. This chapter covers a few of the more common problem scenarios not yet addressed in this book and how you can use Project 2013 to resolve the issues.

Problem: One of My Resources Is Overallocated

Overallocation occurs when a resource in your project is assigned to work that exceeds their available time (the value entered in the resource's **Max Units** field). For example, a resource has a **Max Units** value of 100% for a project. That resource is assigned 75% to one task and 50% to another task at the same time. Because the assignment total is 125%, and the resource's availability is 100%, the resource is overallocated by 25%.

Project 2013 provides a visual indicator when a resource assigned to a task is overallocated. In the **Gantt Chart** view, look for a red icon in the **Indicators** column, as shown in Figure 11.1.

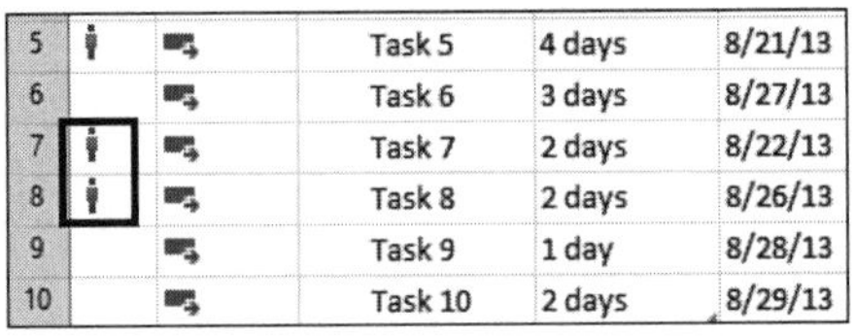

5	👤	▬	Task 5	4 days	8/21/13
6		▬	Task 6	3 days	8/27/13
7	👤	▬	Task 7	2 days	8/22/13
8	👤	▬	Task 8	2 days	8/26/13
9		▬	Task 9	1 day	8/28/13
10		▬	Task 10	2 days	8/29/13

FIGURE 11.1

Look for the highlighted red icons in the Indicators column to identify overallocated resources.

So what do you do if you find that you have overallocated resources in your project? *Resource leveling* is the process of looking at how resources are allocated in your project and moving the assignments around so that tasks are done according to constraints (as soon as possible, for example), but without forcing resources to work beyond 100% of their availability.

Project 2013 enables you to control how leveling occurs in your project. First, make sure that manual leveling is selected for the project. On the **Resource** tab, in the **Level** group, click **Leveling Options**. In the **Resource Leveling** dialog box, under **Leveling Calculations**, ensure that **Manual** is selected, as shown in Figure 11.2.

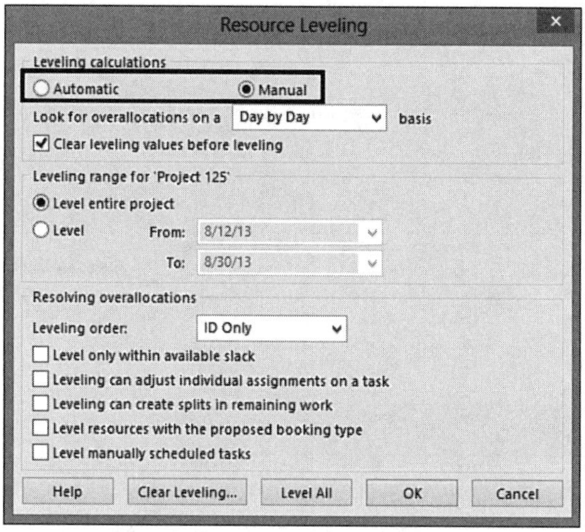

Resource Leveling

Leveling calculations

○ Automatic   ● Manual

Look for overallocations on a Day by Day ▼ basis

☑ Clear leveling values before leveling

Leveling range for 'Project 125'

● Level entire project

○ Level   From: 8/12/13 ▼

            To: 8/30/13 ▼

Resolving overallocations

Leveling order: ID Only ▼

☐ Level only within available slack

☐ Leveling can adjust individual assignments on a task

☐ Leveling can create splits in remaining work

☐ Level resources with the proposed booking type

☐ Level manually scheduled tasks

Help   Clear Leveling...   Level All   OK   Cancel

FIGURE 11.2

Under Leveling Calculations, click Manual.

You have a few different ways to manually level resources in your project.

To level all resources across all tasks in your project, on the **Resource** tab, in the **Level** group, click **Level All**, as shown in Figure 11.3.

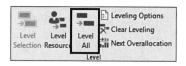

FIGURE 11.3

Click Level All to level all resources in your project.

To level all resources assigned to specific tasks in your project, follow these steps:

1. Press **Ctrl** and click the row header for each task you want to level. This selects the tasks.

2. On the **Resource** tab, in the **Level** group, click **Level Selection**, as shown in Figure 11.4.

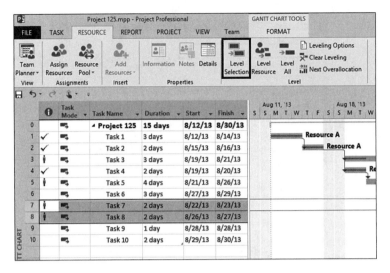

FIGURE 11.4

Select the appropriate tasks, and then click Level Selection.

To level specific resource across all tasks in your project, follow these steps:

1. On the **Resource** tab, in the **Level** group, click **Level Resource**, as shown in Figure 11.5.

FIGURE 11.5

Select the appropriate tasks and then click Level Resource.

2. In the **Level Resource** dialog box, shown in Figure 11.6, click the name of the resource you want to level, and then click **Level Now**.

FIGURE 11.6

Click the name of a resource, and then click Level Now.

If at any point you no longer want resources leveled on your project, on the **Resource** tab, in the **Level** group, click **Clear Leveling**, as shown in Figure 11.7.

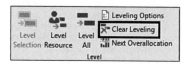

FIGURE 11.7

Click Clear Leveling to remove leveling from your project.

If you have several overallocations that you want to deal with one at a time in a project with many tasks, you can go through the overallocations one at a time by clicking **Next Overallocation** (on the **Resource** tab, in the **Level** group), as shown in Figure 11.8.

FIGURE 11.8

Click Next Overallocation to move to the next issue.

Problem: My Schedule Goes Longer Than My Deadline

This problem is not uncommon. Resources provide updates to tasks in your project, you finish adding those updates to your project, and you find that those updates have pushed out the schedule because the work is being completed slower than scheduled. The last task is now scheduled to finish in November, and you have a deadline of the end of October. Or maybe you included a milestone in your project to represent the deadline, and you see that tasks are going beyond that milestone (as shown in Figure 11.9). Any number of expletives may be running through your head, and you're not sure what you should do to put things back on track.

ⓘ	Task Mode ▾	Task Name ▾	Duration ▾	Start ▾	Finish ▾		
	☴	◢ **Project 125**	**15 days**	**8/12/13**	**8/30/13**		
✓	☴	Task 1	3 days	8/12/13	8/14/13		
✓	☴	Task 2	2 days	8/15/13	8/16/13		
ⅰ	☴	Task 3	3 days	8/19/13	8/21/13		
✓	☴	Task 4	2 days	8/19/13	8/20/13		
ⅰ	☴	Task 5	4 days	8/21/13	8/26/13	Resource B,Resource A	
	☴	Task 6	3 days	8/27/13	8/29/13	Resource B	
ⅰ	☴	Task 7	2 days	8/22/13	8/23/13	rce B	
ⅰ	☴	Task 8	2 days	8/26/13	8/27/13	Resource A	
	☴	Task 9	1 day	8/28/13	8/28/13	Resource A	
	☴	Task 10	2 days	8/29/13	8/30/13	Resource A	
🗓	☴	Deadline	0 days	8/28/13	8/28/13	◆ 8/28	

FIGURE 11.9

An example of a deadline (indicated by a diamond on the Gantt chart) with tasks in the critical path extending beyond it in the Detail Gantt view.

First things first: You need to figure out what factors are tying your schedule down. You can use the Task Inspector (on the **Task** tab, in the **Tasks** group, click **Inspect**) to help identify which of these factors may be contributing to the lengthy schedule:

- **Constraints:** If tasks in your project have constraints applied, review those constraints and make sure that you really need them in place. Does that task really need to start no earlier than that date? Can you make that date a little earlier? Look closely at what you can do to the constraints to save some time in your overall project schedule. For more information on constraints, see Chapter 4, "Working with Tasks."

NOTE The constraints that could cause problems in this case would be **Must Start On**, **Must Finish On**, **Start No Earlier Than**, and **Finish No Earlier Than**. These constraints can often cause tasks to be stuck in time and not be able to pull back if one of their predecessors moves back in time.

- **Dependencies:** Look closely at the dependencies you have set up between tasks in your project. Does one task really need to wait for the next task to finish completely, or can it start when the previous task is 50% done? Do those two tasks really need to finish at the same time, or can one finish a bit earlier so that its successor can get started earlier? Make sure that dependencies accurately reflect what needs to happen in your project. See Chapter 4 for more information on overlapping tasks in your project.

- **Duration:** Are the durations of your tasks accurate, or have you added some padding to the durations to give your resources wiggle room? If you padded your durations, now is the time to take that padding out and be realistic about what you need to get done to finish this project on time. This is a common issue, especially when adding updates from resources to a project. The updates you enter may increase durations, or the actions you take during leveling may push out a finish date. For more information on adjusting task durations, see Chapter 4.

- **Calendars:** This is a tricky one. Remember that you have project, task, and resource calendars to account for. Look at each of these calendars and see how it is affecting the remaining tasks in your project. Is a resource that's assigned to one of the remaining tasks taking a week of vacation in the middle of the task? Can you assign someone else to do the work so that the task can be done sooner? Or can you move the task earlier in the project, before the resource goes on vacation? Evaluate nonworking time in each calendar used by the remaining tasks and see what you can move around to bring in the schedule. For more information on calendars, see the section titled "Setting Up Your Project's Calendars" in Chapter 3, "Starting a Project."

If adjusting constraints, overlapping tasks, shortening durations, and moving tasks around based on calendar availability do not bring your schedule in enough to meet your deadline, you might consider assigning additional resources to your tasks. With more people working on tasks, or more machinery available to do the work, your team might be able to get tasks done more quickly, enabling you to meet your deadline. In thinking about this option, however, it is critical to balance the importance of meeting the deadline with the costs incurred by adding resources to your project. It may make more sense to push the deadline out to a later date. You still incur resource costs because of the additional hours that the existing resources put in past the original deadline, but those costs may be less than the costs incurred by adding more staff or equipment to get the work done on time.

Problem: My Costs Are Exceeding My Budget

You've set a budget for your project, and you've been checking spending against budget regularly, using the processes you learned in Chapter 6, "Accounting for Project Costs." While reviewing costs, you realize that you have now crossed from spending on target to overspending. First, you want to figure out where these overages are coming from.

To identify the source of cost overages in the **Resource Usage** view, follow these steps:

1. On the **View** tab, in the **Resource Views** group, click **Resource Usage**.

2. On the **View** tab, in the **Data** group, click **Budget Assignment** in the **Group by** list.

3. On the **View** tab, in the **Data** group, click **Outline**, and then click **Outline Level 1**. Each of the groupings collapses so that you can easily look at the numbers for each of the budget assignments.

4. Compare the **Budget Cost** column with the **Actual Cost** column, and the **Budget Work** column with the **Actual Work** column. If the actual values are higher than the budget values, that budget assignment contains overages.

> **NOTE** If these columns aren't displayed in the **Resource Usage** view, add them by clicking **Add New Column** on the right side of the table portion of the view. For more information, see the section titled "Adding Values to Budget Resources" in Chapter 6.

5. Click the plus sign next to the name of the budget assignment that contains the overage. This expands the budget assignment, enabling you to review each resource that has that budget assignment.

6. Look through the actual data for each resource, expanding resource names to see task-specific data. Look across the right pane in the view to see time-phased actual cost and work data.

> **NOTE** If the time-phased portion of the view doesn't currently display budget and actual cost and work data, on the **Format** tab, in the **Details** group, click **Add Details**. Use the **Usage Details** tab of the **Detail Styles** dialog box to add these fields to the view.

Also, several visual and basic reports can help you narrow down cost issues, as listed in Table 11.1.

TABLE 11.1 Cost Reports in Project 2013

Excel Reports	Visio Reports	Basic Reports
Cash Flow	Cash Flow	Cash Flow
Earned Value Over Time		Cost Overruns
Resource Cost Summary		Earned Value Report
Baseline Cost		Resource Cost Report
Budget Cost		Task Cost Overview
		Overbudget Tasks

For more information on generating reports, see the "Reporting on Your Project" section of Chapter 8, "Sharing Your Project with Others."

After you've identified where the cost issues are occurring, the next step is deciding what you want to do to get your costs back to budget. Baselining may be a good idea here, so that you capture what your data looks like before making modifications. For more information on baselining, see "Baselining Your Project" in Chapter 7, "Capturing Project Progress."

You can take a few approaches to cut back on costs.

Assigning Work to Fewer People

If you've got any extra resources working on your project, perhaps they can be better used on another project. By removing excess resource assignments from your project, you reduce the costs that those resource assignments incur.

 NOTE Be careful to only remove extra resources, because overloading the remaining resources can lead to exorbitant and unnecessary overtime pay.

For more information on working with resource assignments, see "Assigning Resources to Tasks" in Chapter 5, "Working with Resources."

Cutting Back on What Needs to Get Done

Are there remaining tasks that aren't 100% necessary for completion of your project? By removing tasks, you also remove resource assignments, thereby reducing the associated costs.

For more information on working with tasks, see Chapter 4.

Trimming Budget Amounts

Are you sure that your budget amounts are accurate? If you've padded your budget a bit for flexibility, now is the time to cinch up the belt and be realistic. Sometimes, all that's needed is a more realistic set of budget data to get your project back on track.

For more information on adjusting budget data, see "Adding Values to Budget Resources" in Chapter 6.

THE ABSOLUTE MINIMUM

Problems are going to arise in your use of Project 2013. Schedules are complex things and Project 2013 can be confusing at times, particularly for those that are new to how it works. This chapter provides some solutions for a few issues you might face, but the key to learning the tool to the point where you can fix your own issues (and maybe even avoid some from the beginning) is to play around with the tool before jumping into managing your first big project. Read through the chapters in this book. Create some test projects and work with the options and settings and get to know how the tool works before you begin your project.

APPENDIX

GUIDE TO PROJECT FIELDS

Fields

Task Fields

Task fields display in Usage views and on the Task forms and within the Task Information dialog.

Name	Scope	Description/Usage
Active	Task	The field is used to mark a task as being active or inactive. An inactive task (Active field set to No) shows up in task-based views but in a dimmed font and with a strike-through. These tasks do not contribute to work, cost, or date rollups and do not appear on the critical path. This is useful for creating contingency plan tasks or for removing tasks that have been canceled or removed from the project scope without having to delete them completely.
Actual Cost	Task	If actual costs are set to be calculated by Microsoft Project, this field contains the costs already actually accrued by resources on the task plus the portion of fixed costs accrued according to the Fixed Cost Accrual field. If actual costs are *not* calculated by Project, it contains the value manually entered by the project manager. This field is used by the earned value calculations to determine the to-date costs of the task.
Actual Duration	Task	The number of working periods (shown in days by default) between the actual start date of the task and the latest actual work or the point to which task percent complete has been marked.
Actual Finish	Task	The date on which the task was completed.
Actual Overtime Cost	Task	This field is read-only at the task level. It shows the task-level rollup of the assignment level actual overtime costs from all the resource assignments on the task. Overtime work (and by extension overtime) costs are an assignment-level feature.

Name	Scope	Description/Usage
Actual Overtime Work	Task	This field is read-only at the task level. It shows the task-level rollup of the assignment level actual overtime work from all the resource assignments on the task. Overtime work is an assignment-level feature.
Actual Start	Task	This field shows the date and time that a task or an assignment actually began, based on progress information that you entered.
Actual Work	Task	The amount of work (shown in hours by default) that has actually been completed on the task. If resources are assigned to the task, this will, by default, be the sum of the assignment-level Actual Work fields. With no resources assigned, it is manually entered by the project manager. Note: If resources are assigned and you type a number into the task-level Actual Work field, the value you enter is spread across the assigned resources according to proportion of their assignment units.
ACWP	Task	ACWP stands for actual cost of work performed and is part of the calculations of earned value in Project. ACWP is the actual cost of the task up to the project status date. This means that the ACWP for a task can be lower than the actual cost of the task if the status date is prior to the point up to which the task is complete.
Assignment Delay	Task	This field does not show any data at the task level.
Assignment Units	Task	This field does not show any data at the task level.
Baseline Budget Cost	Task	This field is a copy (at the point in time when the baseline was saved) of the budget cost of the project. It captures only the cost associated with budget resources. This field shows up for all displayed tasks, but it contains a value for the Project Summary task only, because only the Project Summary task can have a budget cost.

Name	Scope	Description/Usage
Baseline Budget Work	Task	This field is a copy (at the point in time when the baseline was saved) of the budget work of the project. It captures only the cost associated with budget resources. This field shows up for all displayed tasks, but it contains a value for the Project Summary task only, because only the Project Summary task can have budget work.
Baseline Cost	Task	This field is a copy (at the point in time when the baseline was saved) of the task Cost field. Baseline cost is used by the earned value calculations.
Baseline Deliverable Finish	Task	This field is a copy of the value of the task Deliverable Finish field (at the time that the baseline was saved). A deliverable is a feature that is available only in Project Server, so this field is visible only when using Project 2013 Professional.
Baseline Deliverable Start	Task	This field is a copy of the value of the task Deliverable Start field (at the time that the baseline was saved). A deliverable is a feature that is available only in Project Server, so this field is visible only when using Project 2013 Professional.
Baseline Duration	Task	This field is a copy (at the point in time when the baseline was saved) of the task Duration field.
Baseline Estimated Duration	Task	If the Task Mode field is set to Auto Scheduled, then when the baseline is saved this field is a copy of the task Duration field. If the Task Mode field is set to Manually Scheduled and the task Duration field is blank, this field is set to 1 day when you save the baseline. If the task Duration field is not blank, this field contains the duration value at the time the baseline was saved.

Name	Scope	Description/Usage
Baseline Estimated Finish	Task	If the Task Mode field is set to Auto Scheduled, when the baseline is saved this field is a copy of the task Finish field.
		If the Task Mode field is set to Manually Scheduled and the task Start and Finish fields are blank, this field is set to the Project start date.
		If the Finish field contains a date, then at the time the baseline is saved this field is a copy of the finish date. If the Finish field is blank, but the Start field contains a value, this field is a copy of the start date.
Baseline Estimated Start	Task	If the Task Mode field is set to Auto Scheduled when the baseline is saved, then this field is a copy of the task Start field.
		If the Task Mode field is set to Manually Scheduled and the task Start and Finish fields are blank, this field is set to the Project start date.
		If the Start field contains a date, then at the time the baseline is saved this field is a copy of the start date. If the Start field is blank but the Finish date contains a value, this field is a copy of the finish date.
Baseline Finish	Task	This field is a copy (at the point in time when the baseline was saved) of the task Finish field.
Baseline Start	Task	This field is a copy (at the point in time when the baseline was saved) of the task Start field.
Baseline Work	Task	This field is a copy (at the point in time when the baseline was saved) of the task Work field.
Baseline1-10 Budget Cost	Task	This field is a copy (at the point in time when the baseline was saved) of the budget cost of the project. It only captures the cost associated with budget resources. This field shows up for all displayed tasks, but it is only showing a value for the Project Summary task because only the Project Summary task can have budget cost.

Name	Scope	Description/Usage
Baseline1-10 Budget Work	Task	This field is a copy (at the point in time when the baseline was saved) of the budget work of the project. It captures the cost associated only with budget resources. This field shows up for all displayed tasks, but it is showing a value only for the Project Summary task because only the Project Summary task can have budget work.
Baseline1-10 Cost	Task	This field is a copy (at the point in time when the baseline was saved) of the task Cost field. Baseline cost is used by the earned value calculations.
Baseline1-10 Deliverable Finish	Task	This field is a copy of the value of the task Deliverable Finish field (at the time that the baseline was saved). A deliverable is a feature that is available only in Project Server, so this field is visible only when using Project 2013 Professional.
Baseline1-10 Deliverable Start	Task	This field is a copy of the value of the task Deliverable Start field (at the time that the baseline was saved). A deliverable is a feature that is available only in Project Server, so this field is visible only when using Project 2013 Professional.
Baseline1-10 Duration	Task	This field is a copy (at the point in time when the baseline was saved) of the task Duration field.
Baseline1-10 Estimated Duration	Task	If the Task Mode field is set to Auto Scheduled, when the baseline is saved this field is a copy of the task Duration field. If the Task Mode field is set to Manually Scheduled and the task Duration field is blank, this field is set to 1 day when you save the baseline. If the Duration field is not blank, this field contains the duration value at the time the baseline was saved.

Name	Scope	Description/Usage
Baseline1-10 Estimated Finish	Task	If the Task Mode field is set to Auto Scheduled, then when the baseline is saved this field is a copy (at the point in time when the baseline was saved) of the task Finish field. If the Task Mode field is set to Manually Scheduled and the task Start and Finish fields are blank, this field is set to the project start date. If the Finish field contains a date at the time the baseline is saved, this field is a copy of the finish date. If the Finish field is blank but the Start field contains a value, this field is a copy of the start date.
Baseline1-10 Estimated Start	Task	If the Task Mode field is set to Auto Scheduled, then when the baseline is saved this field is a copy of the task Start field. If the Task Mode field is set to Manually Scheduled and the task Start and Finish fields are blank, this field is set to the project start date. If the Start field contains a date, then at the time the baseline is saved this field is a copy of the start date. If the Start field is blank but the Finish date contains a value, this field is a copy of the finish date.
Baseline1-10 Finish	Task	This field is a copy (at the point in time when the baseline was saved) of the task Finish field.
Baseline1-10 Start	Task	This field is a copy (at the point in time when the baseline was saved) of the task Start field.
Baseline1-10 Work	Task	This field is a copy (at the point in time when the baseline was saved) of the task Work field.
BCWP (widely known also as EV or Earned Value)	Task	BCWP is calculated by multiplying the BCWS of a task by the task percent complete up to the project status date. This value tells you how much money your baseline plan said it was going to cost to do the amount of work you have actually done on the task.

Name	Scope	Description/Usage
BCWS (widely known also as PV or Planned Value)	Task	BCWS is the portion of the task baseline cost value taken up to the project status date. This value tells you how much money your baseline said it was going to cost to do the work scheduled to be performed between the task start and the current project status date.
Budget Cost	Task	This field displays the sum of all the assignment-level budget cost values for all budget cost resources assigned to the Project Summary task. This field shows up for all displayed tasks, but it contains a value only for the Project Summary task, because only the Project Summary task can have budget cost.
Budget Work	Task	This field displays the sum of all the assignment-level budget work values for all budget work resources assigned to the Project Summary task. This field shows up for all displayed tasks, but it contains a value only for the Project Summary task, because only the Project Summary task can have budget work.
Constraint Date	Task	This field displays the date related to the value in the Constraint Type field. This field will be NA if the constraint type is As Soon as Possible or As Late as Possible.
Constraint Type	Task	This field contains the current constraint associated with the task. If the value is anything other than As Soon as Possible or As Late as Possible, this field should be read with the Constraint Date field as that field contains the date that is related to the constraint type.
Contact	Task	This field is a text field used by some organizations to hold the name or information about the person responsible for the task.
Cost	Task	This field contains the total cost value for the task. If a task has no resource assignments, this field can be manually edited to contain the projected cost of the task. If a task has resources assigned, this field is the sum of the assignment-level cost values from those assignments plus the value of the task field called Fixed Cost.

Name	Scope	Description/Usage
Cost Rate Table	Task	At the task level, this field is available for views but contains no data. It is an assignment-level field only.
Cost Variance	Task	This field is the difference between the baseline cost and the cost of a task. Calculated: Cost variance = Cost – Baseline cost
Cost1-10	Task	These fields enable you to store your own custom cost values for tasks. Note: Resources and assignments also have Cost1-10 fields, but they do not "roll up" to the task level.
CPI	Task	This field displays the calculated ratio between baseline cost performed and the actual cost of work performed. Calculated: CPI = BCWP \ ACWP A CPI that is equal to or greater than 1 is good. One means the task is progressing exactly to plan from a cost perspective. Greater than 1 means that it is coming in under budget. A CPI that is less than 1 means that the task is costing more than was planned.
Created	Task	This field contains the date/time that the task was created.
Critical	Task	This field indicates if the task Total Slack field is equal to or less than 0. The field will equal Yes if the task Total Slack is 0 or less and will equal No if it is greater than 0. It is generally accepted that tasks where Critical equals Yes (on the critical path) are more important to pay attention to because any slip in those tasks will result in the project finish date also slipping.
CV	Task	This field displays the difference between baseline cost of performed and the actual cost of work performed. Calculated: CPI = BCWP – ACWP. A CV greater than 0 means that the project is under budget.

Name	Scope	Description/Usage
CV%	Task	CV% is the ratio between CV and BCWP and is calculated as follows: CV% = ((BCWP – ACWP) / BCWP) * 100 The CV field shows you the dollar value of how much over or under budget you are up to the status date. The CV% field shows you the same data but as a percentage of BCWP.
Date1-10	Task	These fields enable you to store your own custom date values for tasks. You can use these fields when you need to track a date that relates to the task but is not a date that Project already tracks with a built-in field.
Deadline	Task	This field contains the date past which the task finish should not exceed. Deadlines allow users to track a "drop dead" date without having to use a Must Finish On constraint. If the finish date of the task goes past the deadline date, an indicator is shown in the Indicators column. Note: A deadline date may change the way that total slack is calculated for the task and could impact the critical path of the project.
Deliverable Finish	Task	For a task that has a deliverable linked to it, this field contains the scheduled finish date of the linked deliverable. Deliverables are a feature of Project Server, and this field is available only in Project Professional.
Deliverable GUID	Task	For a task that has a deliverable linked to it, this field contains the GUID (globally unique identifier) of the linked deliverable. Deliverables are a feature of Project Server, and this field is available only in Project Professional.

Name	Scope	Description/Usage
Deliverable Name	Task	For a task that has a deliverable linked to it, this field contains the name of the linked deliverable. Deliverables are a feature of Project Server, and this field is available only in Project Professional.
Deliverable Start	Task	For a task that has a deliverable linked to it, this field contains the scheduled start date of the linked deliverable. Deliverables are a feature of Project Server, and this field is available only in Project Professional.
Deliverable Type	Task	If the task has no linked deliverables, this field contains a 0. If the task is the source of the deliverable to which it is linked, the field contains a 1. If the deliverable to which the task is linked has been produced by some other task, the field contains a 2. Deliverables are a feature of Project Server, and this field is available only in Project Professional.
Duration	Task	This field shows the number of working periods (working as defined by the calendars that impact the task) between the start and finish dates. If the task has splits, the splits are not included in the duration value. By default, this is displayed in days.
Duration Variance	Task	The field is the difference between duration and baseline duration and is calculated as follows: Duration variance = Duration − Baseline duration This field is useful when trying to see if there are tasks that are taking longer than your baseline plan had scheduled. You can insert this field and then filter on it to show only nonzero values to quickly show all tasks that are taking longer than scheduled.
Duration1-10	Task	These fields enable you to store your own custom duration values for tasks.

Name	Scope	Description/Usage
EAC (Estimate at Completion)	Task	This field shows the projected total task cost given the actual performance of the task cost up to the project Status Date. Calculated: EAC = ACWP + (Baseline Cost − BCWP) / CPI In earlier versions, this field was just a simple cost of the Cost field. It is now a true projection that takes task performance into account.
Early Finish	Task	This field shows the earliest date that the task could finish. This takes into account predecessor/successor early finish dates as well as leveling delays and constraints. Early Finish is used in calculating the critical path of the project.
Early Start	Task	This field shows the earliest date that the task could start. This takes into account predecessor/successor early start dates as well as leveling delays and constraints. Early Start is used in calculating the critical path of the project.
Earned Value Method	Task	This field contains the method that Project will use to calculate BCWP for the task. The options are % Complete and Physical % Complete.
Effort Driven	Task	This field shows if the task is set to use effort-driven scheduling.
Error Message	Task	This field shows resource and project import error messages that occur during the Project Server Import Resources to Enterprise or Import Project to Enterprise Wizards. It is visible only in Project Professional.
Estimated	Task	This field shows if the task duration is flagged as an estimate. This field controls the display of the question mark indicator in the Duration field. If this field is set to Yes, the duration will have a question mark next to it to indicate that the number is seen as an estimate.

Name	Scope	Description/Usage
External Task	Task	This field contains a Yes value if the task is part of a cross-project link and is the task in the link that is from another file.
Finish	Task	This field is the date the task is scheduled to be completed.
Finish Slack	Task	This field is the difference between the late finish and early finish. By default, this is displayed in days. Calculated: Finish slack = Late finish − Early finish
Finish Variance	Task	This field shows the difference between the task finish and the baseline finish. It is used to show if the task is scheduled to finish earlier or later than originally scheduled. Calculated: Finish variance = Finish − Baseline finish A positive number means that the task is scheduled to finish later than expected.
Finish1-10	Task	This field can be used to store custom finish data.
Fixed Cost Accrual	Task	This field displays the method used to calculate how much of the fixed cost value should be added into the actual cost of the task. If set to Start, the total of the Fixed Cost field is added to the actual cost of the task as soon as % complete is greater than 0. If set to Prorated, the Fixed Cost value is multiplied by % complete, and the result is added to actual cost. If set to End, the total of the Fixed Cost field is added to the actual cost of the task as soon as % complete is 100.
Fixed Cost	Task	Allows the user to enter costs associated with the task that are not directly resource related. The value of this field is added to the Cost field for the task and is added to the actual cost of the task based on the accrual method found in the Fixed Cost Accrual method field.
Flag1-20	Task	These custom fields allow users to store their own Yes/No values for the task.

Name	Scope	Description/Usage
Free Slack	Task	The working time that a task can be delayed without impacting the schedule of any of its successors. Not to be confused with total slack, which is the time that a task can be delayed without affecting the finish date of the project as a whole.
Group By Summary	Task	In a view that is grouped using the Group By functionality on the View tab of the ribbon, this field indicates if a particular row in the view is a task or if it is the summary row that represents all the members of a grouping.
Health	Task	This field is used only with Project Server, and is used as a subjective indicator of the state of the task. The Project Server administrator can customize the available values for this field.
Hide Bar	Task	This field sets whether a bar should appear on Gantt Chart or Calendar views for the task. If set to No (the default), a bar shows in these views for the task. If Yes, the bar is hidden.
ID	Task	The ID field is automatically generated by Project and assigned to each task. The number is *not* persistent, however. Certain acts by the user can cause the ID fields to be reassigned during sorting. The ID field should *not* be used as a way to refer to tasks over time. The unique ID should be used for any long-term references to tasks.
Ignore Resource Calendar	Task	If set to Yes, Project will not take the resource calendar working and nonworking time information into account when scheduling the task.
Indicators	Task	This field displays various icons that represent information or warnings about the task. These can include indications of any constraints on the task, if the task is behind schedule, if it is complete, and whether the finish date is past the deadline date.
Late Finish	Task	This field is the latest the task finish date can slip before it impacts the finish date of the project.

Name	Scope	Description/Usage
Late Start	Task	This field is the latest the task start date can slip before it impacts the finish date of the project.
Level Assignments	Task	The resource-leveling functionality in Project can be set to allow it to adjust individual assignments on a task to level resource allocations. If this field is set to No, the leveling feature will *not* be allowed to adjust assignments on that task.
Leveling Can Split	Task	If this field is set to No, the leveling functionality in Project cannot put splits in the remaining portion of the task to level resource allocations. This *greatly* limits the ability of Project to level possible overallocations.
Leveling Delay	Task	The amount of time that the task start (or the remaining portion of the task) has been delayed due to the resource-leveling features.
Marked	Task	This field can be used by the project manager for any purpose that requires a task to be "marked" in some way. It has no built-in functionality other than the fact that a marked task can have its own Gantt bar formatting.
Milestone	Task	If the field is set to Yes, Project sees this task as a milestone. Setting the Duration field to 0 will automatically change this field to Yes.
Name	Task	This field contains the description or name of the task. The task name should generally contain both verbs and nouns.
Notes	Task	This field contains rich text data that describes or pertains to the task.
Number1-20	Task	These custom fields allow users to store their own numeric values for the task.
Outline Code1-10	Task	These custom fields allow users to store custom data that pertains to the task that draw from multilevel, hierarchical value lists. These hierarchies can then be used to summarize task data based on the structure of the hierarchy.

Name	Scope	Description/Usage
Outline Level	Task	This field indicates the indentation level of the task in the project outline structure. The Project Summary task is always Outline Level = 0. All top-level summary tasks are level 1.
Outline Number	Task	This field is a hierarchical representation of the task's position relative to other tasks. For example, the first task would be 1. The first child task of task 1 would be 1.1. The second child task of 1 would be 1.2.
Overallocated	Task	Yes if the task is part of an over-allocation of one of its assigned resources. Overallocated means that the resource is assigned to do more work in a given time period than their availability settings dictate is possible.
Overtime Cost	Task	This field shows the sum of the overtime costs for the resources assigned to the task.
Overtime Work	Task	This field shows the sum of the overtime work for the resources assigned to the task.
% Complete	Task	The portion of the scheduled duration that is actually completed Calculated: % Complete = Actual duration / Duration
% Work Complete	Task	The portion of the scheduled work that is completed. Calculated: % Work complete = Actual work / Work
Physical Percent Complete	Task	A manually entered value that represents how much of the task has been completed. This field is often used instead of % Complete to calculate BCWP.
Placeholder	Task	A Yes value indicates that the manually scheduled task is missing either the start or finish dates.
Predecessors	Task	This field displays the task ID and link information for the tasks that are linked to the current task as predecessors.

Name	Scope	Description/Usage
Preleveled Finish	Task	This field displays the value of the task Finish field before a resource-leveling action was performed.
Preleveled Start	Task	This field displays the value of the task Start field before a resource-leveling action was performed.
Priority	Task	This field displays the leveling priority for the task. When you are using priority-based resource leveling, the value of this field is used to determine which tasks should be moved first. A higher number means the task will be moved later than a lower-numbered task. A value of 1000 means that the task will not be moved at all.
Project	Task	This field displays the name of the project to which the task or inserted project belongs.
Publish	Task	This field is used only when using Project Server. With it, the project manager can selectively publish task and assignment information for certain tasks when publishing the project to Project Server. If the field is set to No, that task will *not* be published to the server.
Recurring	Task	This field displays whether the task is a recurring task.
Regular Work	Task	This field displays the number of hours (hours by default) of work that are *not* overtime. Calculated: Regular work = Work – Overtime work
Remaining Cost	Task	This field displays the total amount of cost for the remaining portion of the task. Calculated: Remaining cost = Cost – Actual cost The actual calculation is as follows: Remaining cost = (Remaining work * Resource standard rate) + Remaining overtime cost
Remaining Duration	Task	This field displays time periods (days by default) left to complete the task. Calculated: Remaining duration = Duration – Actual duration

Name	Scope	Description/Usage
Remaining Overtime Cost	Task	This field displays the cost of the remaining portion of overtime work on the task. Calculated: Remaining overtime cost = Remaining overtime work * Resource overtime rate
Remaining Overtime Work	Task	This field displays the number of hours of scheduled overtime left to complete the task. Calculated: Remaining overtime work = Overtime work – Actual overtime work
Remaining Work	Task	This field displays the hours of work left to complete the task. Calculated: Remaining work = Work – Actual work
Resource Group	Task	This field displays the values of the Resource Group fields for the resources assigned to the task.
Resource Initials	Task	This field displays the values of the Resource Initials fields for the resources assigned to the task.
Resource Names	Task	This field displays the resource names assigned to the task. If the resource is assigned at less than their max units values, the originally entered assignment units for that resource are displayed here also.
Resource Phonetics	Task	In the Japanese language version of Project, this field displays the Hiragana or Katakana for the resources assigned to the task
Resource Type	Task	This field displays the type of the resources assigned to the task. This field is best used in the Task Usage view. In a Gantt Chart view, this field is blank.
Response Pending	Task	This field displays Yes if a response from an assigned resource is pending after having sent updates to resources.
Resume	Task	For an in-progress task, this field displays the date that the unfinished portion of the task starts. For example, if a 10-day duration task starts on Day 1 and is 50% complete, the resume date would be Day 6.

Name	Scope	Description/Usage
Rollup	Task	If set to Yes for a subtask, the parent summary task displays a bar for that subtask on the summary task Gantt bar. This is useful for displaying the distribution of subtasks over time directly on the summary task Gantt bar.
Scheduled Duration	Task	For an automatically scheduled task, this field is the same as the Duration field. For a manually scheduled task that does not have enough data to calculate a normal duration yet still has resources assigned to do work across several days, this field displays the number of days that work is scheduled to be done by those resources.
Scheduled Finish	Task	For an automatically scheduled task, this field is the same as the Finish field. For a manually scheduled task without enough data to calculate a finish date yet still has resources assigned to do work, this field indicates the last date on which these resources are scheduled to work.
Scheduled Start	Task	For an automatically scheduled task, this field is the same as the Start field. For a manually scheduled task without enough data to calculate a start date yet still has resources assigned to do work, this field indicates the first date on which these resources are scheduled to work.
SPI (Schedule Performance Index)	Task	This field displays the amount of budgeted cost performed compared to the budgeted cost of the work scheduled. Calculated: SPI = BCWP / BCWS A value of 1 or higher is preferable, with a value of 1 meaning exactly on schedule and higher than 1 meaning ahead of schedule.
Start	Task	This field is the date the task is scheduled to start.

Name	Scope	Description/Usage
Start Slack	Task	This field is the difference between the early start and late start dates for the task. Calculated: Start slack = Late start – Early start The lesser of the start slack and finish slack values for the task determines the free slack value, which is the duration that a task can be delayed before it impacts the start of a successor task.
Start Variance	Task	This field is the difference between the start and baseline start of a task. Calculated: Start variance = Start – Baseline start This field lets the scheduler see if changes to the schedule are impacting the intended start dates of tasks.
Start1-10	Task	This field is the start date of Interim Plan 1-10. Can be used to store custom start data. These fields are also used by the interim plan functionality on the Save Baseline dialog. When an interim plan is saved (in the Save Baseline dialog), the start and finish dates of the tasks are copied into StartX\FinishX.
Status	Task	This field displays a text-based status indication of the task. If the Start field is greater than the project Status Date, this field shows Future Task. If the completed portion of the task is up to the day before the project status date (or later), the field shows On Schedule. If the completed portion of the task is *not* up to at least the day before the project status date, the field shows Late. If the task is 100% complete, the field shows Complete.
Status Indicator	Task	This field displays an icon that represents the value of the Status field.

Name	Scope	Description/Usage
Status Manager	Task	This field displays the name of the Project Server user that is responsible for approving status updates submitted by resources on this task.
		By default, this is the user that created the task even if that user is *not* the project owner of the project.
Stop	Task	This field displays the date and time where the actual portion of the task ends.
		The Stop field is generally immediately prior to the date in the Resume field.
Subproject File	Task	For a row that represents an inserted project, this field displays the path to the source project for the inserted project file.
Subproject Read Only	Task	For a row that represents an inserted project, this field indicates if the inserted project was inserted read only. If read only then the field contains Yes.
Successors	Task	This field displays the task ID and link information for the tasks that are linked to the current task as successors.
Summary	Task	This field displays if the current task is a summary task. If it is a summary task, this field contains Yes.
		This field can be used to create filters to show or not show summary tasks in a view.
Summary Progress	Task	This field is not visible in the table portion of views. It can be used when defining bar styles for Gantt bars.
		It allows a bar style to be created that is to summary bars what Complete Through is for normal tasks.
SV (Schedule Variance)	Task	This field displays the difference between the BCWP and BCWS fields.
		SV = BCWP − BCWS
		A value of 1 or higher is good. One means the task is exactly on schedule. Higher than 1 means ahead of schedule.

Name	Scope	Description/Usage
SV%	Task	This field shows the proportion of schedule variance to BCWS. It is displayed as a % value. Calculated: SV% = (SV / BCWS) * 100 A value of 0 or higher is good. 0% means the task is on schedule. Higher than 0% means it is ahead of schedule.
Task Calendar	Task	This field displays the calendar that has been applied to the task. If this field contains None, no calendar is applied. If this field displays the name of a calendar and the option for Scheduling Ignores Resource Calendars, the displayed calendar alone drives the scheduling of the task.
Task Calendar GUID	Task	This field contains the GUID value for the calendar that is applied to the task in the Task Calendar field.
Task GUID	Task	This field displays the GUID value for the task. GUIDs are useful when having to identify tasks across projects where the ID or Unique ID (unique IDs are unique within a project) fields could be the same. The GUID will be unique to a task even across projects.
Task Mode	Task	This field controls whether the task is manually scheduled or automatically scheduled. The default when installing Project 2013 is manually scheduled.
TCPI (To Complete Performance Index)	Task	This field is the proportion of the remaining work and the remaining cost from the status date to the end of the task. Calculated: TCPI = (BAC – BCWP) / (BAC – ACWP) A value of 1 or *less* is a good thing. If the value is greater than 1, you must complete work faster to stay within budget.

Name	Scope	Description/Usage
Text1-Text30	Task	These fields provide the user with 30 different 256-character fields to be used for any purpose. The best uses for these fields are for capturing task-level information that is specific to your project or organization that is not already captured by an out-of-the-box field within Project 2013. This might be the location of a task or how the task lines up to a requirements document or capturing some special instructions about the task. Like other custom fields, these can be renamed and can even use formula or lookup tables to control the values entered.
Total Slack	Task	The duration (in days by default) that a task could slip before it delayed the finish date of the entire project. A value of 0 means that the task is on the critical path and cannot move at all. Any delay in the finish of the task would delay the project. For tasks with values greater than 0 this field is useful for monitoring how close a task is to being critical. A task with a total slack value of 100 days likely needs to be monitored less than a task with a total slack value of 2 days.
Type	Task	This field indicates if the task is fixed units, fixed work, or fixed duration. Task type allows the user to have some control over how Project will perform the Duration = Work/Units calculation by "fixing" one of the elements.
Unique ID	Task	Automatically generated integer that Project 2013 assigns to a task when it is created. Unlike the ID, the Unique ID does not change over the life of the project. Within a project, this field is completely unique and will not be reused even if tasks are deleted.
Unique ID Predecessors	Task	This field is the same as the Predecessors field, but it uses the Unique ID instead of the ID.
Unique ID Successors	Task	This field is the same as the Successors field, but it uses the Unique ID instead of the ID.

Name	Scope	Description/Usage
VAC	Task	The difference between the baseline cost and the EAC (estimate at completion). Calculated: EAC = Baseline cost – EAC A value of 0 means the task is exactly on track. A positive value means that you are on track to be under budget.
Warning	Task	The Warning field shows if Project sees an issue with the start date, finish date, or duration of a manually scheduled task. This could include links to other tasks or task constraints. This field will work in conjunction with a red underline in the field with the potential issue.
WBS (Work Breakdown Structure)	Task	This field contains the work breakdown structure for the task. By default, the WBS is the same as the outline number of the task but can be customized to display specialized coding structures that can be used to link tasks to specific elements in requirements documents or other organizationally specific structures.
WBS Predecessors	Task	The same as the Predecessors field, but instead of the ID field it identifies the predecessors with their WBS value.
WBS Successors	Task	The same as the Successors field, but instead of the ID field it identifies the successors with their WBS value.
Work	Task	The amount of time (expressed in hours by default) that will be spent by all the assigned resources performing the task over the course of the task duration.
Work Contour	Task	This field indicates the predefined distribution of work over the duration of the task. By default this is Flat, but the choices allow for the work to be front loaded, back loaded, and so on according to several predefined distributions.

Name	Scope	Description/Usage
Work Variance	Task	The difference between the baseline work and the work for the task.
		Calculated: Work variance = Work – Baseline work
		A positive number here means that more work is currently on the task than was originally planned in the baseline.

Task-Timephased Fields

Task-timephased fields display on the right side of Usage views.

Field	Scope	Description
Actual Cost (Timephased)	Task	This field displays the actual cost for the task, broken down by time period.
		This field is visible in task Usage views only and is useful for determining how the total task actual cost breaks out over time.
Actual Fixed Cost (Timephased)	Task	This field displays the actual fixed cost for the task, broken down by time period.
		This field is visible in task Usage views only and is useful for determining how the total task actual fixed cost breaks out over time.
Actual Overtime Work (Timephased)	Task	This field displays the actual overtime work for the task, broken down by time period.
		This field is visible in task Usage views only and is useful for determining how the total task actual overtime work breaks out over time.
Actual Work (Timephased)	Task	This field displays the actual work for the task, broken down by time period.
		This field is visible in task Usage views only and is useful for determining how the total task actual work breaks out over time.
ACWP (Timephased)	Task	This field displays the ACWP for the task, broken down by time period.
		This field is visible in task Usage views only and is useful for determining how the total task ACWP breaks out over time.
Baseline Budget Cost (Timephased)	Task	This field displays the baseline budget cost for the project Summary task, broken down by time period.
		This field is visible in task Usage views and only for the Project Summary task and is useful for determining how the baseline budget cost breaks out over time.

Field	Scope	Description
Baseline Budget Work (Timephased)	Task	This field displays the baseline budget work for the Project Summary task, broken down by time period. This field is visible in task Usage views and only for the Project Summary task and is useful for determining how the baseline budget work breaks out over time.
Baseline Cost (Timephased)	Task	This field displays the baseline cost for the task, broken down by time period. This field is visible in task Usage views only and is useful for determining how the total task baseline cost breaks out over time. This field, in conjunction with the timephased-task Cost and Actual Cost fields, can be used to make time-based comparisons between planned, current, and actual costs for the project.
Baseline Work (Timephased)	Task	This field displays the baseline work for the task, broken down by time period. This field is visible in task Usage views only and is useful for determining how the total task baseline work breaks out over time. This field, in conjunction with the timephased-task Work and Actual Work fields, can be used to make time-based comparisons between planned, current, and actual work for the project.
Baseline0-10 Cumulative Work (Timephased)	Task	This field displays the running total of the baseline work values for the task. This means that for any time period the value of this field is the sum of the baseline work of all prior periods and the current period for that particular baseline.
Baseline0-10 Remaining Cumulative Work (Timephased)	Task	This field contains the running total of the amount of remaining work according to the baseline in question. This means that if a task had a baseline of 80 hours at 8 hours a day the baseline remaining cumulative work for the first day would be 80 and on the second day it would be 72 (because the baseline shows 8 hours per day).

Field	Scope	Description
Baseline0-10 Remaining Tasks (Timephased)	Task	This field displays the number of tasks that are remaining to be completed on a given day according to the particular baseline. This field is calculated for all tasks but is really only valuable for summary tasks where it can help the user determine how many tasks should have been completed according to the baseline. Use this field in conjunction with the Remaining Tasks field.
Baseline1-10 Budget Cost (Timephased)	Task	This field displays the Baseline1-10 budget cost for the Project Summary task, broken down by time period. This field is visible in task Usage views and only for the Project Summary task and is useful for determining how the Baseline1-10 budget cost breaks out over time.
Baseline1-10 Budget Work (Timephased)	Task	This field displays the Baseline1-10 budget work for the Project Summary task, broken down by time period. This field is visible in task Usage views and only for the Project Summary task and is useful for determining how the Baseline1-10 budget work breaks out over time.
Baseline1-10 Cost (Timephased)	Task	This field displays the Baseline1-10 cost, broken down by time period. This field is visible in task Usage views and only for the Project Summary task and is useful for determining how the Baseline1-10 cost breaks out over time.
Baseline1-10 Work (Timephased)	Task	This field displays the Baseline1-10 work, broken down by time period. This field is visible in task Usage views and only for the Project Summary task and is useful for determining how the Baseline1-10 work breaks out over time.
BCWP (Timephased)	Task	This field displays the BCWP for the task, broken down by time period. This field is visible in task Usage views only and is useful for determining how the total task BCWP breaks out over time.

Field	Scope	Description
BCWS (Timephased)	Task	This field displays the BCWS for the task, broken down by time period. This field is visible in task Usage views only and is useful for determining how the total task BCWS breaks out over time.
Budget Cost (Timephased)	Task	This field displays the budget cost for the Project Summary task, broken down by time period. This field is visible in task Usage views and only for the Project Summary task and is useful for determining how the budget cost breaks out over time.
Budget Work (Timephased)	Task	This field displays the budget cost for the Project Summary task, broken down by time period. This field is visible in task Usage views and only for the Project Summary task and is useful for determining how the budget cost breaks out over time.
Cost (Timephased)	Task	This field displays the cost for the task, broken down by time period. This field is visible in task Usage views only and is useful for determining how the total task cost breaks out over time.
CPI (Timephased)	Task	This field displays the CPI for the task, broken down by time period. This field is visible in task Usage views only and is useful for determining how the total task CPI breaks out over time.
Cumulative Actual Work (Timephased)	Task	This field displays the running total of the actual work by time period. Each time period for this field will contain the sum of the actual work for the current time period and all previous time periods.
Cumulative Cost (Timephased)	Task	This field displays the running total of the cost by time period. Each time period for this field will contain the sum of the cost for the current time period and all previous time periods.

Field	Scope	Description
Cumulative % Complete (Timephased)	Task	This field displays the running total of the % Complete field by time period. Each time period for this field will contain how complete the task was at the end of that time period.
Cumulative Work (Timephased)	Task	This field displays the running total of the work by time period. Each time period for this field will contain the sum of the work for the current time period and all previous time periods.
CV (Timephased)	Task	This field displays the CV for the task, broken down by time period. This field is visible in task Usage views only and is useful for determining how the total task CV breaks out over time.
CV% (Timephased)	Task	This field displays the CV% for the task, broken down by time period. This field is visible in task Usage views only and is useful for determining how the total task CV% breaks out over time.
Fixed Cost (Timephased)	Task	This field displays the fixed cost for the task, broken down by time period. This field is visible in task Usage views only and is useful for determining how the total task fixed cost breaks out over time.
Overtime Work (Timephased)	Task	This field displays the overtime work for the task, broken down by time period. This field is visible in task Usage views only and is useful for determining how the total task overtime work breaks out over time.
% Complete (Timephased)	Task	This field contains the current total % complete of the task. This field is not really timephased. It displays the same value for every time period.

Field	Scope	Description
Regular Work (Timephased)	Task	This field displays the regular work for the task, broken down by time period. This field is visible in task Usage views only and is useful for determining how the total task regular work breaks out over time. Calculated: Regular work = Work – Overtime work
Remaining Actual Tasks (Timephased)	Task	This field displays the number of tasks that are remaining to be completed on a given day according to the currently scheduled start and finish dates. This field is calculated for all tasks but is really only valuable for summary tasks where it can help the user determine how many tasks should have been completed according to the baseline. Use this field in conjunction with the Baseline Remaining Tasks and Remaining Tasks fields.
Remaining Cumulative Work (Timephased)	Task	This field displays the running total of the remaining work by time period. Each time period for this field will contain the total remaining work as of that time period.
Remaining Tasks (Timephased)	Task	This field displays the number of tasks that are scheduled to be completed on a given day according to the currently scheduled start and finish dates. This field is calculated for all tasks but is really only valuable for summary tasks where it can help the user determine how many tasks should have been completed according to the baseline.
SPI (Timephased)	Task	This field displays the SPI for the task, broken down by time period. This field is visible in task Usage views only and is useful for determining how the total task SPI breaks out over time.
SV (Timephased)	Task	This field displays the SV for the task, broken down by time period. This field is visible in task Usage views only and is useful for determining how the total task SV breaks out over time.

Field	Scope	Description
SV% (Timephased)	Task	This field displays the SV% for the task, broken down by time period. This field is visible in task Usage views only and is useful for determining how the total task SV% breaks out over time.
Work (Timephased)	Task	This field displays the work for the task, broken down by time period. This field is visible in task Usage views only and is useful for determining how the total task work breaks out over time.

Resource Fields

Resource fields are displayed in Usage views and on the Task forms as well as within the Resource Information dialog.

Field	Scope	Description
Accrue At	Resource	This field controls how costs for the resource are to be spread out over the duration of their task assignments. The default is Prorated, which spreads costs out evenly over the duration.
Actual Cost	Resource	This field contains the costs already actually accrued by resources on their assigned tasks plus the portion of task fixed costs accrued according to the Fixed Cost Accrual field.
Actual Finish	Resource	Used in resource Usage views to display the date an assignment actually finished.
Actual Overtime Cost	Resource	This field is read-only at the resource-level. It shows the resource-level rollup of the assignment-level actual overtime costs from all the task assignments on the resource. Overtime work (and by extension overtime costs) is an assignment-level feature.
Actual Overtime Work	Resource	This field is read-only at the resource level. It shows the task-level rollup of the assignment-level actual overtime work from all the task assignments on the task. Overtime work is an assignment-level feature.
Actual Start	Resource	This field, when inserted into a resource Usage view, shows the date and time that an assignment actually began, based on progress information that you entered.
Actual Work	Resource	The amount of work (shown in hours by default) that has actually been completed on the task. In Resource views, this field is read-only.
ACWP	Resource	ACWP stands for actual cost of work performed, and this field is part of the calculations of earned value in Project. ACWP is the actual cost of the resources, task assignments up to the project status date.

Field	Scope	Description
Assignment	Resource	Useful only in resource Usage views, the Assignment field indicates whether the row is an assignment row instead of a resource row.
Available From	Resource	The date from which the resource can work on tasks. Use this field if you have a resource that will join your team after the project begins. Project will mark a resource as overallocated if you assign a task prior to the available-from date.
Available To	Resource	The date up to which the resource can work on tasks. Use this field if you have a resource that will be leaving the project before the project is complete. Project marks a resource as overallocated if you assign a task after the available-to date.
Base Calendar	Resource	This field is the shared calendar on which the resource calendar is based. The resource working time is defined by the combination of the base calendar and the exceptions added to the resource calendar.
Baseline Budget Cost	Resource	This field is a copy (at the point in time when the baseline was saved) of the budget cost associated with a particular budget resource.
Baseline Budget Work	Resource	This field is a copy (at the point in time when the baseline was saved) of the budget work associated with a particular budget resource.
Baseline Cost	Resource	This field is a copy (at the point in time when the baseline was saved) of the task Cost field.
Baseline Finish	Resource	This field is a copy (at the point in time when the baseline was saved) of the task Finish field.
Baseline Start	Resource	This field is a copy (at the point in time when the baseline was saved) of the task Start field.
Baseline Work	Resource	This field is a copy (at the point in time when the baseline was saved) of the task Work field.

Field	Scope	Description
Baseline1-10 Budget Cost	Resource	This field is a copy (at the point in time when the baseline was saved) of the budget cost of the particular budget resource.
Baseline1-10 Budget Work	Resource	This field is a copy (at the point in time when the baseline was saved) of the budget work of the particular budget resource.
Baseline1-10 Cost	Resource	This field is a copy (at the point in time when the baseline was saved) of the task Cost field. Baseline cost is used by the earned value calculations.
Baseline1-10 Finish	Resource	These fields store the planned completion date for the resource, at the time that you save a corresponding baseline.
Baseline1-10 Start	Resource	These fields store the planned start date for the resource, at the time that you save a corresponding baseline.
Baseline1-10 Work	Resource	These fields store the planned working time for the resource, at the time that you save a corresponding baseline.
BCWP	Resource	BCWP is calculated by multiplying the BCWS of a resource's task assignments by the task % complete values, up to the project status date. This value tells you how much money your baseline plan said it was going to cost to do the amount of work you have actually done on the tasks assigned to the resource.
BCWS	Resource	BCWS is the portion of the resource's task assignment baseline cost values taken up to the project status date. This value tells you how much money your baseline said it was going to cost to do the work scheduled to be performed between the task assignments start and the current project status date.
Budget	Resource	This field defines if a resource is a budget resource. The value is set to Yes if the resource is to be used to track high-level project cost and work budgets.
Budget Cost	Resource	For budget resources, this field displays the sum of all the assignment-level budget cost values for the resource.

Field	Scope	Description
Budget Work	Resource	For budget resources, this field displays the sum of all the assignment-level budget work values for the resource.
Can Level	Resource	This field determines if the resource-leveling features of Project will be allowed to act upon the resource. If set to No, resource leveling will not act upon the resource's assignments.
Code	Resource	This field can contain any custom data about the resource. It has no functionality within Project itself.
Cost	Resource	This field contains the sum of all the task assignment cost values for the resource.
Cost Per Use	Resource	The value of this field is added to the cost of each assignment of the resource to a task. This is useful for tracking such costs as the delivery charges of a piece of equipment.
Cost Rate Table	Resource	When inserted into a resource Usage view this field shows the cost rate table that is in force for a given assignment.
Cost Type	Resource	This field is available only when using Project in conjunction with Project Server 2013. This field allows the Project Server administrator to define specific cost types and then to assign these types to specific enterprise resources.
Cost Variance	Resource	This field is the difference between the baseline cost and the cost of a resource. Calculated: Cost variance = Cost – Baseline cost
Cost1-10	Resource	These fields enable you to store your own custom cost values for resources.
Created	Resource	This field is the date/time that the resource was added to the project team.

Field	Scope	Description
CV	Resource	This field displays the difference between baseline cost of work performed and the actual cost of work performed. Calculated: CPI = BCWP − ACWP
Date1-10	Resource	These fields enable you to store your own custom date values for resources. You can use these fields when you need to track a date that relates to the resource but is not a date that Project already tracks with a built-in field.
Default Assignment Owner	Resource	This is a Project Server 2013 field that defines which Project Server user will be responsible for providing status updates on the tasks assigned to this resource. By default, it is the resource themselves that is the default assignment owner. Set this field to a different user if resources will *not* be providing their own status updates via Project Server. An example of this is a resource that is not connected to your network and cannot access Project Server.
Duration1-10	Resource	These fields enable you to store your own custom duration values for resources. You can use these fields when you need to track a duration that relates to the resource but is not a duration that Project already tracks with a built-in field.
E-mail Address	Resource	This field stores the email address for the resource.
Enterprise	Resource	This field displays if the resource is part of the Project Server enterprise resource pool or a local resource. If the value is Yes, the resource is part of the enterprise pool.
Enterprise Base Calendar	Resource	This field displays Yes if the resource's base calendar is an enterprise calendar.
Enterprise Required Values	Resource	This field displays Yes if all the required enterprise fields have been supplied for the resource.

Field	Scope	Description
Enterprise Team Member	Resource	This field indicates if a resource is a member of the current project team or if the resource is a team member on another enterprise project that is currently open in Project Professional. If the value is Yes, the resource is on the team for the active project. If No, the resource is a team member on another open project.
Enterprise Unique ID	Resource	The unique ID generated by Project Server to distinguish between resources.
Error Message	Resource	This field is used only in the Import Resources to Enterprise Wizard to display import error information.
Finish1-10	Resource	These fields enable you to store your own custom finish or date values for resources. You can use these fields when you need to track a date that relates to the resource but is not a date that Project already tracks with a built-in field.
Finish	Resource	The latest assignment finish date among all the task assignments for the resource.
Flag1-20	Resource	These fields enable you to store your own custom Yes/No data values for resources.
Generic	Resource	This field determines if a resource is generic. If a resource is generic, it represents an entire class or type of resource within your organization, not a specific resource.
Group	Resource	User definable field for associating a resource with a custom group.
ID	Resource	The ID field is automatically generated by Project and assigned to each resource. The number is *not* persistent, however. Certain acts by the user can cause the ID fields to be reassigned during sorting. The ID field should *not* be used as a way to refer to resources over time. The unique ID should be used for any long-term references to resources.

Field	Scope	Description
Import	Resource	This field is used only during the Import Resource to Enterprise Wizard and indicates if the user wants to import the resource into the enterprise resource pool.
Inactive	Resource	This field indicates if the enterprise resource is an active member of the enterprise resource pool. If a user is deleted from Project Server, that user's corresponding resource is marked as inactive so that project managers can no longer assign them to tasks.
Indicators	Resource	This field displays various icons that represent information or warnings about the resource.
Initials	Resource	This field allows the user to capture the initials of the resource.
Material Label	Resource	If the resource is a material, this field displays how the resource unit values display in other views in Project. For example, if the material is sand, the label might be pounds. Then, if you assign 500 of that resource to a task, it shows up as 500 pounds.
Max Units	Resource	This field is the units value past which the resource will be seen by Project to be overallocated. If a resource calendar defines their working day as 10 hours a day and their max units value is 80%, Project will mark them as overallocated if the sum of their task assignments for a day becomes greater than 80% of their 10 hour day, or 8 hours.
Name	Resource	This field is the name of the resource.
Notes	Resource	This field contains rich text data that describes or pertains to the task.
Number1-20	Resource	These fields enable you to store your own custom number values for resources.
Objects	Resource	This field is the number of embedded objects related to the resource.
Outline Code1-10	Resource	These fields enable you to store your own custom hierarchical data values for resources.

Field	Scope	Description
Overallocated	Resource	This field displays if Project has determined that the resource is overallocated.
Overtime Cost	Resource	This field shows the sum of the overtime costs for the resource task assignments.
Overtime Rate	Resource	This field is the rate Project will use to calculate the overtime costs associated with this resource on tasks and assignments.
Overtime Work	Resource	This field shows the sum of the overtime work for the resource's task assignments.
Peak	Resource	This field is the highest units value for any time period across all the resource's task assignments.
% Work Complete	Resource	This field is the portion of the scheduled work that is actually complete. Calculated: % Work complete = Actual work / work
Project	Resource	This field is the project to which the resource is associated.
RBS	Resource	This field is a Project Server enterprise resource field that associates the resource to a resource breakdown structure as defined by the Project Server administrator. The RBS field can be directly associated with the security model with Project Server.
Regular Work	Resource	This field displays the number of hours (hours by default) of work that are *not* overtime. Calculated: Regular work = Work − Overtime work
Remaining Cost	Resource	This field displays the total amount of cost for the remaining portion of the resource's task assignments. Calculated: Remaining cost = Cost − Actual cost The actual calculation is as follows: Remaining cost = (Remaining work * Resource standard rate) + Remaining overtime cost

Field	Scope	Description
Remaining Overtime Cost	Resource	This field displays the cost of the remaining portion of overtime work on the resource's task assignments. Calculated: Remaining Overtime Cost = Remaining Overtime Work * Resource Overtime Rate
Remaining Overtime Work	Resource	This field displays the number of hours of scheduled overtime left to complete the resource's task assignments. Calculated: Remaining overtime work = Overtime work – Actual overtime work
Remaining Work	Resource	This field displays the hours of work left to complete the resource's task assignments. Calculated: Remaining work = Work – Actual work
Resource Departments	Resource	For a Project Server enterprise resource, this field displays the Project Server departments to which this resource is associated.
Standard Rate	Resource	This field is the rate Project uses to calculate nonovertime resource costs.
Start	Resource	This field is the earliest of the resource's assignment start dates.
Start1-10	Resource	These fields enable you to store your own custom start or date values for resources.
SV	Resource	This field displays the difference between the BCWP and BCWS fields. Calculated: SV = BCWP – BCWS
Team Assignment Pool	Resource	When you are using Project Server, this field indicates if the resource represents a team assignment pool.

Field	Scope	Description
Text1-30	Resource	These fields provide the user with 30 different 256-character fields to be used for any purpose.
		The best uses for these fields are for capturing resource-level information that is specific to your project or organization that is not already captured by an out-of-the-box field within Project 2013.
		Like other custom fields, these can be renamed and can even use formula or lookup tables to control the values entered.
Type	Resource	This field indicates the type of the resource. The choices are Cost, Work, and Material.
Unique ID	Resource	This field is the automatically generated integer that Project 2013 assigns to a resource when it is created. Unlike the ID, the Unique ID does not change over the life of the project. Within a project, this field is completely unique and will not be reused even if resources are deleted.
Update Needed	Resource	This field indicates that resource task assignments have changed to the point where the resource should be updated on the new data.
VAC	Resource	The difference between the baseline cost and the EAC (estimate at completion).
		Calculated: EAC = Baseline cost – EAC
		A value of 0 means that the resource's task assignments are exactly on track. A positive value means that you are on track to be under budget.
Windows User Account	Resource	This field displays the Active Directory account information for the resource.
Work	Resource	This field is the amount of time (expressed in hours by default) that will be spent by the resource on all their assigned tasks.

Field	Scope	Description
Work Variance	Resource	This field is the difference between the baseline work and the work for the resource's task assignments.
		Calculated: Work variance = Work – Baseline work
		A positive number here means that more work is currently on the tasks than was originally planned in the baseline.

Resource-Timephased Fields

Resource-timephased fields display on the right side of the Usage view.

Field	Field Scope	Description
Actual Cost (Timephased)	Resource	This field displays the actual cost for the resource, broken down by time period. This field is visible in resource Usage views only and is useful for determining how the total resource actual cost breaks out over time.
Actual Overtime Work (Timephased)	Resource	This field displays the actual overtime work for the resource, broken down by time period. This field is visible in resource Usage views only and is useful for determining how the total resource actual overtime work breaks out over time.
Actual Work (Timephased)	Resource	This field displays the actual work for the resource, broken down by time period. This field is visible in resource Usage views only and is useful for determining how the total resource actual work breaks out over time.
ACWP (Timephased)	Resource	This field displays the ACWP for the resource, broken down by time period. This field is visible in resource Usage views only and is useful for determining how the total resource ACWP breaks out over time.
Baseline Budget Cost (Timephased)	Resource	For a budget cost resource, this field displays the baseline budget cost broken down by time period. This field is visible in resource Usage views and only for the Project Summary task and is useful for determining how the baseline budget cost breaks out over time.
Baseline Budget Work (Timephased)	Resource	For a budget work resource, this field displays the baseline budget work broken down by time period. This field is visible in resource Usage views and only for the Project Summary task and is useful for determining how the baseline budget work breaks out over time.

Field	Field Scope	Description
Baseline Cost	Resource	This field displays the baseline cost for the resource, broken down by time period.
		This field is visible in resource Usage views only and is useful for determining how the total resource baseline cost breaks out over time.
		This field, in conjunction with the timephased Cost and Actual Cost fields, can be used to make time-based comparisons between planned, current, and actual costs for the resource.
Baseline Work	Resource	This field displays the baseline work for the resource, broken down by time period.
		This field is visible in resource Usage views only and is useful for determining how the total resource baseline work breaks out over time.
		This field, in conjunction with the timephased Work and Actual Work fields, can be used to make time-based comparisons between planned, current, and actual work for the resource.
Baseline0-10 Cumulative Work (Timephased)	Resource	These fields display the running total of the baseline work values for the resource's task assignments. This means that for any time period the value of this field is the sum of the baseline work of all prior periods and the current period for that particular baseline.
Baseline0-10 Remaining Cumulative Work (Timephased)	Resource	These fields contain the running total of the amount of remaining work according to the baseline in question. This means that if a resource's task assignments had a baseline of 80 hours at 8 hours a day the baseline remaining cumulative work for the first day would be 80 and on the second day it would be 72, because the baseline shows 8 hours per day.

Field	Field Scope	Description
Baseline1-10 Budget Cost (Timephased)	Resource	For a Budget cost resource, these fields display the Baseline1-10 budget cost for the Project Summary task, broken down by time period. These fields are visible in resource Usage views and only for the Project Summary task and are useful for determining how the Baseline1-10 budget cost breaks out over time.
Baseline1-10 Budget Work (Timephased)	Resource	For a budget work resource, these fields display the Baseline1-10 budget work, broken down by time period. These fields are visible in resource Usage views and only for the Project Summary task and are useful for determining how the Baseline1-10 budget work breaks out over time.
Baseline1-10 Cost (Timephased)	Resource	These fields display the Baseline1-10 cost broken down by time period. These fields are visible in resource Usage views and only for the Project Summary task and are useful for determining how the Baseline1-10 cost breaks out over time.
Baseline1-10 Work (Timephased)	Resource	These fields display the Baseline1-10 work, broken down by time period. These fields are visible in resource Usage views and only for the Project Summary task and are useful for determining how the Baseline1-10 work breaks out over time.
BCWP (Timephased)	Resource	This field displays the BCWP for the resource, broken down by time period. This field is visible in resource Usage views only and is useful for determining how the total BCWP breaks out over time.
BCWS (Timephased)	Resource	This field displays the BCWS for the resource, broken down by time period. This field is visible in resource Usage views only and is useful for determining how the total BCWS breaks out over time.

Field	Field Scope	Description
Budget Cost (Timephased)	Resource	For a budget cost resource, this field displays the budget cost for the Project Summary task, broken down by time period. This field is visible in resource Usage views and only for the Project Summary task and is useful for determining how the budget cost breaks out over time.
Budget Work (Timephased)	Resource	For a budget work resource, this field displays the budget cost for the Project Summary task, broken down by time period. This field is visible in resource Usage views and only for the Project Summary task and is useful for determining how the budget cost breaks out over time.
Cost (Timephased)	Resource	This field displays the cost for the resource, broken down by time period. This field is visible in resource Usage views only and is useful for determining how the total task cost breaks out over time.
Cumulative Actual Work (Timephased)	Resource	This field displays the running total of the actual work by time period. Each time period for this field will contain the sum of the actual work for the current time period and all previous time periods.
Cumulative Cost (Timephased)	Resource	This field displays the running total of the cost by time period. Each time period for this field will contain the sum of the cost for the current time period and all previous time periods.
Cumulative Work (Timephased)	Resource	This field displays the running total of the work by time period. Each time period for this field will contain the sum of the work for the current time period and all previous time periods.
CV (Timephased)	Resource	This field displays the CV for the resource, broken down by time period. This field is visible in resource Usage views only and is useful for determining how the total CV breaks out over time.

Field	Field Scope	Description
Overtime Work (Timephased)	Resource	This field displays the overtime work for the resource, broken down by time period. This field is visible in resource Usage views only and is useful for determining how the total overtime work breaks out over time.
Peak Units (Timephased)	Resource	This field displays the peak units value for a given time period.
% Allocation (Timephased)	Resource	This field displays the sum of the resource assignment units value for a given time period.
Regular Work (Timephased)	Resource	This field displays the regular work for the resource, broken down by time period. This field is visible in resource Usage views only and is useful for determining how the total regular Work breaks out over time. Calculated: Regular work = Work – Overtime work
Remaining Availability (Timephased)	Resource	This field displays the number of hours a resource has left to work on tasks after they have worked on their existing task assignments for a given time period. Calculated: Remaining availability = Work availability – Work
Remaining Cumulative Actual Work (Timephased)	Resource	This field displays the running total of the remaining work for tasks left to be completed by time period.
Remaining Cumulative Work (Timephased)	Resource	This field displays the running total of the remaining work by time period. Each time period for this field will contain the total remaining work as of that time period.
SV (Timephased)	Resource	This field displays the SV for the resource, broken down by time period. This field is visible in resource Usage views only and is useful for determining how the total SV breaks out over time.
Unit Availability (Timephased)	Resource	This field displays the max units value for a resource for a given time period.

Field	Field Scope	Description
Work (Timephased)	Resource	This field displays the work for the resource, broken down by time period. This field is visible in resource Usage views only and is useful for determining how the total work breaks out over time.
Work Availability (Timephased)	Resource	This field displays the number of hours a resource is available to work on tasks for a given time period.

Assignment Fields

Assignment fields display in Usage views and on the Task forms and within the Assignment Information dialog.

Field	Scope	Description
Actual Cost	Assignment	If actual costs are set to be calculated by Microsoft Project, this field contains the costs already actually accrued by resources on the task plus the portion of fixed costs accrued according to the Fixed Cost Accrual field. If actual costs are *not* calculated by Project, it contains the value manually entered by the project manager.
Actual Finish	Assignment	This field is the date on which the task was completed.
Actual Overtime Cost	Assignment	This field shows the assignment-level actual overtime costs.
Actual Overtime Work	Assignment	This field is the assignment-level actual overtime work.
Actual Start	Assignment	This field shows the date and time that the assignment actually began, based on progress information that you entered.
Actual Work	Assignment	This field shows the amount of work (shown in hours by default) that has actually been completed on the assignment.
ACWP	Assignment	ACWP stands for actual cost of work performed and is part of the calculations of earned value in Project. ACWP is the actual cost of the assignment up to the project status date. This means that the ACWP for an assignment can be lower than the actual cost of the task if the status date is prior to the point up to which the assignment is complete.
Assignment Owner	Assignment	This field is the name of the Project Server user that is responsible for entering updates into Project Server for the assignment.
Assignment Units	Assignment	This field is the percentage of the assigned resource's full working day that they are working on the assignment.

Field	Scope	Description
Baseline Budget Cost	Assignment	This field is a copy (at the point in time when the baseline was saved) of the budget cost of the project. It only captures the cost associated with budget resources. This field shows up for all displayed tasks, but it contains a value only for the Project Summary task, because only the Project Summary task can have budget cost.
Baseline Budget Work	Assignment	This field is a copy (at the point in time when the baseline was saved) of the budget work of the project. It only captures the cost associated with budget resources. This field shows up for all displayed tasks, but it contains a value only for the Project Summary task, because only the Project Summary task can have budget work.
Baseline Cost	Assignment	This field is a copy (at the point in time when the baseline was saved) of the task Cost field. Baseline cost is used by the earned value calculations.
Baseline Finish	Assignment	This field is a copy (at the point in time when the baseline was saved) of the assignment Finish field.
Baseline Start	Assignment	This field is a copy (at the point in time when the baseline was saved) of the assignment Start field.
Baseline Work	Assignment	This field is a copy (at the point in time when the baseline was saved) of the assignment Work field.
Baseline1-10 Budget Cost	Assignment	These fields are copies (at the point in time when the baseline was saved) of the budget cost of the assignment. They only capture the cost associated with budget resources.
Baseline1-10 Budget Work	Assignment	These fields are copies (at the point in time when the baseline was saved) of the budget work of the assignment. They only capture the cost associated with budget resources.
Baseline1-10 Cost	Assignment	These fields are copies (at the point in time when the baseline was saved) of the task Cost field. Baseline cost is used by the earned value calculations.

Field	Scope	Description
Baseline1-10 Estimated Finish	Assignment	If the Task Mode field is set to Auto Scheduled, then when the baseline is saved this field is a copy of the task Finish field.
		If the Task Mode field is set to Manually Scheduled and the task Start and Finish fields are blank, this field is set to the Project start date.
		If the Finish field contains a date, then at the time the baseline is saved this field is a copy of the finish date. If the Finish field is blank but the Start date contains a value, this field is a copy of the start date.
Baseline1-10 Estimated Start	Assignment	If the Task Mode field is set to Auto Scheduled, then when the baseline is saved this field is a copy of the task Start field.
		If the Task Mode field is set to Manually Scheduled and the task Start and Finish fields are blank, this field is set to the Project Start Date.
		If the Start field contains a date, then at the time the baseline is saved this field is a copy of the start date. If the Start field is blank but the Finish date contains a value, this field is a copy of the finish date.
Baseline1-10 Finish	Assignment	These fields are a copy (at the point in time when the baseline was saved) of the assignment Finish field.
Baseline1-10 Start	Assignment	These fields are a copy (at the point in time when the baseline was saved) of the assignment Start field.
Baseline1-10 Work	Assignment	These fields are a copy (at the point in time when the baseline was saved) of the assignment Work field.
BCWP (widely known also as EV or Earned Value)	Assignment	BCWP is calculated by multiplying the BCWS of an assignment by the assignment percent complete up to the project status date. This value tells you how much money your baseline plan said it was going to cost to do the amount of work you have actually done on the assignment.

Field	Scope	Description
BCWS (widely known also as PV or Planned Value)	Assignment	BCWS is the portion of the assignment Baseline Cost value taken up to the project status date. This value tells you how much money your baseline said it was going to cost to do the work scheduled to be performed between the assignment start and the current project status date.
Budget Cost	Assignment	This field displays the sum of all the assignment-level budget cost values for all budget Cost resources assigned to the Project Summary task. This field shows up for all displayed tasks, but it contains a value only for the Project Summary task, because only the Project Summary task can have budget cost.
Budget Work	Assignment	This field displays the sum of all the assignment-level budget work values for all budget work resources assigned to the Project Summary task. This field shows up for all displayed tasks, but it contains a value only for the Project Summary task, because only the Project Summary task can have budget work.
Cost	Assignment	This field contains the total cost value for the assignment.
Cost Rate Table	Assignment	This field indicates which of the resource cost rate tables is in effect for the assignment.
Cost Variance	Assignment	This field is the difference between the baseline cost and the cost of a task. Calculated: Cost variance = Cost − Baseline cost
Cost1-10	Assignment	These fields enable you to store your own custom cost values for assignments.
Critical	Assignment	This field indicates if the task (associated with the assignment) Total Slack field is equal to or less than 0. The field will equal Yes if the task total slack is 0 or less and will equal No if it is greater than 0. It is generally accepted that tasks where Critical equals Yes (on the critical path) are more important to pay attention to because any slip in those tasks will result in the project finish date also slipping.

Field	Scope	Description
CV	Assignment	This field displays the difference between baseline cost of performed and the actual cost of work performed. Calculated: CPI = BCWP – ACWP A CV greater than 0 means that the assignment is under budget.
Date1-10	Assignment	These fields enable you to store your own custom date values for assignments. You can use these fields when you need to track a date that relates to the assignment but is not a date that Project already tracks with a built-in field.
Finish	Assignment	The date the assignment is scheduled to be completed.
Finish Variance	Assignment	This field shows the difference between the assignment finish and the baseline finish. It is used to show if the assignment is scheduled to finish earlier or later than originally scheduled. Calculated: Finish variance = Finish – Baseline finish A positive number means that the assignment is scheduled to finish later than expected.
Finish1-10	Assignment	The fields show the finish date of Interim Plan 1-10. Can be used to store custom finish data. These fields are also used by the interim plan functionality on the Save Baseline dialog. When an interim plan is saved (in the Save Baseline dialog), the start and finish dates of the tasks are copied into StartX\FinishX.
Flag1-20	Assignment	These custom fields allow users to store their own Yes/No values for the assignment.
Leveling Delay	Assignment	This field shows the amount of time that the assignment start (or the remaining portion of the assignment) has been delayed due to the resource-leveling features.
Notes	Assignment	This field contains rich text data that describes or pertains to the assignment.

Field	Scope	Description
Number1-20	Assignment	These custom fields allow users to store their own numeric values for the assignment.
Overallocated	Assignment	Yes if the assignment is part of an overallocation of its assigned resources. *Overallocated* means that the resource is assigned to do more work in a given time period than their availability settings dictate is possible.
Overtime Cost	Assignment	This field shows the sum of the overtime costs for the resources assigned to the assignment.
Overtime Work	Assignment	This field shows the sum of the overtime work for the resources assigned to the assignment.
Peak	Assignment	This field is the highest assignment unit value at any point in the duration of the assignment.
% Work Complete	Assignment	This field is the portion of the scheduled work that is completed. Calculated: % work complete = Actual work / Work
Priority	Assignment	This field displays the leveling priority for the task. When you are using priority-based resource leveling, the value of this field is used to determine which tasks should be moved first. A higher number means the task will be moved later than a lower numbered task. A value of 1000 means that the task will not be moved at all. For an assignment the priority value is the same as the task priority.
Project	Assignment	This field displays the name of the project to which the assignment belongs.
Regular Work	Assignment	This field displays the number of hours (hours by default) of work that are *not* overtime. Calculated: Regular work = Work – Overtime work

Field	Scope	Description
Remaining Cost	Assignment	This field displays the total amount of cost for the remaining portion of the assignment. Calculated: Remaining cost = Cost – Actual cost The actual calculation is as follows: Remaining cost = (Remaining work * Resource standard rate) + Remaining overtime cost
Remaining Overtime Cost	Assignment	This field displays the cost of the remaining portion of overtime work on the assignment. Calculated: Remaining overtime cost = Remaining overtime work * Resource overtime rate
Remaining Overtime Work	Assignment	This field displays the number of hours of scheduled overtime left to complete the assignment. Calculated: Remaining overtime work = Overtime work – Actual overtime work
Remaining Work	Assignment	This field displays the hours of work left to complete the assignment. Calculated: Remaining work = Work – Actual work
Resource Group	Assignment	This field shows the value of the Resource Group field for the resource on the assignment.
Resource ID	Assignment	This field shows the ID for the resource on the assignment.
Resource Initials	Assignment	This field shows the initials for the resource on the assignment.
Resource name	Assignment	This field shows the resource name of the resource on the assignment.
Resource Type	Assignment	This field shows the type of the resource on the assignment.
Start	Assignment	This field shows the date the assignment is scheduled to start.

Field	Scope	Description
Start Variance	Assignment	This field shows the difference between the start and baseline start of an assignment. Calculated: Start variance = Start − Baseline start This field lets the scheduler see if changes to the schedule are impacting the intended start dates of assignments.
Start1-10	Assignment	These fields can be used to store custom start data.
SV	Assignment	This field displays the difference between the BCWP and BCWS fields. Calculated: SV = BCWP − BCWS A value of 1 or higher is good. One means the assignment is exactly on schedule. Higher than 1 means ahead of schedule.
Task ID	Assignment	This field shows the ID of the task associated with the assignment.
Task Name	Assignment	This field shows the name of the task associated with the assignment.
Task Outline Number	Assignment	This field shows the outline number of the task associated with the assignment.
Task Summary	Assignment	This field shows the summary parent name of the task associated with the assignment.
Text1-Text30	Assignment	These fields provide the user with 30 different 256-character fields to be used for any purpose.
Unique ID	Assignment	This field is the automatically generated integer that Project 2013 assigns to an assignment when it is created. Unlike the ID, the Unique ID does not change over the life of the project. Within a project, this field is completely unique and will not be reused even if assignments are deleted.

Field	Scope	Description
VAC	Assignment	This field shows the difference between the baseline cost and the EAC (estimate at completion). Calculated: EAC = Baseline cost – EAC A value of 0 means that the task is exactly on track. A positive value means that you are on track to be under budget.
WBS	Assignment	This field shows the WBS value of the task associated with the assignment.
Work	Assignment	This field shows the amount of time (expressed in hours by default) that will be spent by all the assigned resources performing the assignment over the course of the assignment duration.
Work Contour	Assignment	This field indicates the predefined distribution of work over the duration of the assignment. By default, this is Flat, but the choices allow for the work to be front loaded, back loaded, and so on according to several predefined distributions.
Work Variance	Assignment	This field shows the difference between the baseline work and the work for the assignment. Calculated: Work variance = Work – Baseline work A positive number here means that more work is currently on the assignment than was originally planned in the baseline.

Assignment-Timephased Fields

Assignment-timephased fields display on the right side of the Usage view.

Field	Scope	Description
Actual Cost (Timephased)	Assignment	This field displays the actual cost for the assignment, broken down by time period. This field is visible in Usage views only and is useful for determining how the total actual cost breaks out over time.
Actual Overtime Work (Timephased)	Assignment	This field displays the actual overtime work for the assignment, broken down by time period. This field is visible in Usage views only and is useful for determining how the total actual overtime work breaks out over time.
Actual Work (Timephased)	Assignment	This field displays the actual work for the assignment, broken down by time period. This field is visible in Usage views only and is useful for determining how the total actual work breaks out over time.
ACWP (Timephased)	Assignment	This field displays the ACWP for the assignment, broken down by time period. This field is visible in Usage views only and is useful for determining how the total ACWP breaks out over time.
Baseline Budget Cost (Timephased)	Assignment	For a budget cost resource, this field displays the baseline budget cost broken down by time period. This field is visible in Usage views and only for the Project Summary task and is useful for determining how the baseline budget cost breaks out over time.
Baseline Budget Work (Timephased)	Assignment	For a budget work resource, this field displays the baseline budget work broken down by time period. This field is visible in Usage views and only for the Project Summary task and is useful for determining how the baseline budget work breaks out over time.

Field	Scope	Description
Baseline Cost	Assignment	This field displays the baseline cost for the assignment, broken down by time period.
		This field is visible in Usage views only and is useful for determining how the total baseline cost breaks out over time.
		This field, in conjunction with the timephased Cost and Actual Cost fields, can be used to make time-based comparisons between planned, current, and actual costs.
Baseline Work	Assignment	This field displays the baseline work for the assignment, broken down by time period.
		This field is visible in Usage views only and is useful for determining how the total baseline work breaks out over time.
		This field, in conjunction with the timephased Work and Actual Work fields, can be used to make time-based comparisons between planned, current, and actual work.
Baseline0-10 Cumulative Work (Timephased)	Assignment	These fields display the running total of the baseline work values for the assignment. This means that for any time period the value of this field is the sum of the baseline work of all prior periods and the current period for that particular baseline.
Baseline0-10 Remaining Cumulative Work (Timephased)	Assignment	These fields contain the running total of the amount of remaining work according to the baseline in question. This means that if an assignment has a baseline of 80 hours at 8 hours a day the baseline remaining cumulative work for the first day is 80 and on the second day it is 72, because the baseline shows 8 hours per day.
Baseline1-10 Budget Cost (Timephased)	Assignment	For a budget cost resource, these fields display the Baseline1-10 budget cost for the Project Summary task, broken down by time period.
		These fields are visible in Usage views and only for the Project Summary task and are useful for determining how the Baseline1-10 budget cost breaks out over time.

Field	Scope	Description
Baseline1-10 Budget Work (Timephased)	Assignment	For a budget work resource, these fields display the Baseline1-10 budget work, broken down by time period. These fields are visible in Usage views and only for the Project Summary task and are useful for determining how the Baseline1-10 budget work breaks out over time.
Baseline1-10 Cost (Timephased)	Assignment	These fields display the Baseline1-10 cost broken down by time period. These fields are visible in Usage views and only for the Project Summary task and are useful for determining how the Baseline1-10 cost breaks out over time.
Baseline1-10 Work (Timephased)	Assignment	These fields display the Baseline1-10 work, broken down by time period. These fields are visible in Usage views and only for the Project Summary task and are useful for determining how the Baseline1-10 work breaks out over time.
BCWP (Timephased)	Assignment	This field displays the BCWP for the assignment, broken down by time period. This field is visible in Usage views only and is useful for determining how the total BCWP breaks out over time.
BCWS (Timephased)	Assignment	This field displays the BCWS for the assignment, broken down by time period. This field is visible in Usage views only and is useful for determining how the total BCWS breaks out over time.
Budget Cost (Timephased)	Assignment	For a budget cost resource, this field displays the budget cost for the Project Summary task, broken down by time period. This field is visible in Usage views and only for the Project Summary task and is useful for determining how the budget cost breaks out over time.

Field	Scope	Description
Budget Work (Timephased)	Assignment	For a budget work resource, this field displays the budget cost for the Project Summary task, broken down by time period. This field is visible in Usage views and only for the Project Summary task and is useful for determining how the budget cost breaks out over time.
Cost (Timephased)	Assignment	This field displays the cost for the assignment, broken down by time period. This field is visible in Usage views only and is useful for determining how the total task cost breaks out over time.
Cumulative Actual Work (Timephased)	Assignment	This field displays the running total of the actual work by time period. Each time period for this field will contain the sum of the actual work for the current time period and all previous time periods.
Cumulative Cost (Timephased)	Assignment	This field displays the running total of the cost by time period. Each time period for this field will contain the sum of the cost for the current time period and all previous time periods.
Cumulative Work (Timephased)	Assignment	This field displays the running total of the work by time period. Each time period for this field will contain the sum of the work for the current time period and all previous time periods.
CV (Timephased)	Assignment	This field displays the CV for the assignment, broken down by time period. This field is visible in Usage views only and is useful for determining how the total CV breaks out over time.
Overtime Work	Assignment	This field contains the amount of overtime scheduled to be performed by all resources assigned to a task, for all tasks assigned to a resource, or by a resource on a task, and charged at the overtime rates of the resources involved.
Peak Units (Timephased)	Assignment	This field displays the peak units value for a given time period.

Field	Scope	Description
% Allocation (Timephased)	Assignment	This field displays the sum of the assignment units value for a given time period.
Regular Work (Timephased)	Assignment	This field displays the regular work for the resource, broken down by time period. This field is visible in Usage views only and is useful for determining how the total regular work breaks out over time. Calculated: Regular work = Work – Overtime work
Remaining Availability (Timephased)	Assignment	This field displays the number of hours a resource has left to work on tasks after they have worked on their existing task assignments for a given time period. Calculated: Remaining availability = Work availability – Work
Remaining Cumulative Actual Work (Timephased)	Assignment	This field displays the running total of the remaining work for tasks left to be completed by time period.
Remaining Cumulative Work (Timephased)	Assignment	This field displays the running total of the remaining work by time period. Each time period for this field will contain the total remaining work as of that time period.
SV (Timephased)	Assignment	This field displays the SV for the assignment, broken down by time period. This field is visible in Usage views only and is useful for determining how the total SV breaks out over time.
Work Availability (Timephased)	Assignment	This field displays the number of hours a resource is available to work on tasks for a given time period.

Index

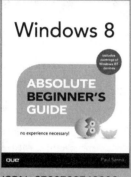
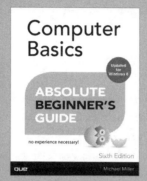
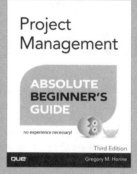

FREE
Online Edition

Your purchase of *Project 2013 Absolute Beginner's Guide* includes access to a free online edition for 45 days through the **Safari Books Online** subscription service. Nearly every Que book is available online through **Safari Books Online**, along with thousands of books and videos from publishers such as Addison-Wesley Professional, Cisco Press, Exam Cram, IBM Press, O'Reilly Media, Prentice Hall, Sams, and VMware Press.

Safari Books Online is a digital library providing searchable, on-demand access to thousands of technology, digital media, and professional development books and videos from leading publishers. With one monthly or yearly subscription price, you get unlimited access to learning tools and information on topics including mobile app and software development, tips and tricks on using your favorite gadgets, networking, project management, graphic design, and much more.

Activate your FREE Online Edition at
informit.com/safarifree

STEP 1:   Enter the coupon code: RQFMNVH.

STEP 2:   New Safari users, complete the brief registration form.
            Safari subscribers, just log in.

If you have difficulty registering on Safari or accessing the online edition,
please e-mail customer-service@safaribooksonline.com